GW00702088

No, Minister!

A radical challenge on economic and
social policies from speeches in
the House of Lords

RALPH HARRIS

General Director,
The Institute of Economic Affairs

Published by
THE INSTITUTE OF ECONOMIC AFFAIRS
1985

First published in February 1985

by

THE INSTITUTE OF ECONOMIC AFFAIRS

2 Lord North Street, Westminster, London SW1P 3LB

ISSN 0073-909X

ISBN 0-255 36179-3

Printed in Great Britain by

GORON PRO-PRINT CO LTD, LANCING, WEST SUSSEX

Filmset Berthold Plantin 11 on 12 point

Contents

Acknowledgements

I AM glad of this opportunity to express the debt I owe my colleague Arthur Seldon and the hundreds of IEA authors whom he assembled and on whose publications I have drawn, largely without acknowledgement, in my writings and speeches for more than a quarter of a century.

I would also like to pay public tribute to the *Hansard* reporters who regularly produce such an accurate record of often imperfectly delivered effusions. Such minimum changes as have been made in this compilation are confined to clarifying the original verbal exposition, modifying inelegancies that jar in written form, and eliminating the elaborate forms of address and references to other speakers which help to civilise debate in the House of Lords.

27 January 1985 RALPH HARRIS

Preface

THE *Occasional Papers* were designed as a series to accommodate texts of the spoken or written word originally addressed to specialist audiences but of wider interest to a larger assembly of readers. The first Occasional Paper was Professor George Stigler's *The Intellectuals and the Market Place* in 1963. Since then 70 have been published.

Number 71 by Lord Harris could be entitled *Legislators and the Market Place*. Professor Stigler analysed the intellectuals' misunderstanding, distrust and antipathy to the market. Lord Harris's speeches to the peers in Parliament are essays in explanation and advocacy that similarly indicate the misunderstanding, distrust and antipathy of peers ranging from seasoned Conservative, Labour and, alas, Liberal politicians to uninstructed bishops. Recent creations provide welcome allies for his campaign of enlightenment.

The task of introducing and appraising this text after a quarter of a century of close partnership with the author is the task that would have faced Gilbert had he been asked to assess Sullivan (or *vice-versa*). These speeches form a fourth phase in Lord Harris's saga of education: from lecturing to students at the University of St Andrews, to informing readers of *The Glasgow Herald*, to enlightening IEA readers in our early collaborations on advertising, hire purchase and welfare and his later *Papers*, and now to entreating, admonishing and trying to persuade a mixed bag of mostly older men and women: heirs or recipients of peerages and bishops. His fourth phase has not, I imagine, been the easiest or most rewarding, for the standard of economic literacy in the Lords does not seem high, even among those who have exercised power in positions of state, and who now stand in judgement on those who follow them, even where in their time they did harm by misdirected policies. There are honourable, if rare, exceptions.

The substance of the 15 speeches between April 1981 and

May 1984 assembled here display Lord Harris's gifts, which would have singled him out for distinction whatever work chance had led him to do. I think of him as a football centre-forward deftly picking up passes, thinking fast on his feet, outwitting the opposing fullbacks by clever dribbling, and distracting goalkeepers with jokes while shooting straight into the goal. The material is well-researched, tolerant in general tone, shot with gentle irony, and mostly temperate in language except when exceptional obtuseness provokes a flash of anger. From the cross-benches he is disappointed or impatient with the Government or Conservative peers (he speaks of 'Tory rustics and romantics' who oppose economies in government spending and reduced taxation), saddened by the clerical sophists who confuse motives with results, all the more because of his practising Christianity, and aroused by symptom-swatting Liberal simplicities and Labour fallacies, although I detect a shadow of hopeful sympathy with the Social Democrats, or rather with what they may one day do.

The edited speeches comprise instructive, entertaining and spirited reading for commoners, from students to entrepreneurs, as well as for peers. They show economics to be far from the dismal science. The 'national economic assessment' urged by Labour is dismissed as 'a pow-wow with the highwayman'. The National Plan 'mocked nature by passing from teething troubles in 1965 to death rattles in 1966 without the customary interval of hopeful life'.

The theme throughout is the consequences of abandoning classical economic liberalism and the urgency of applying its principles to policy in our day. The specific is that Britain's post-war discontents arise not from the use of the market but from its neglect in almost every part of the economy from the labour market, housing and coalmining to the sale of spectacles and public-house licensing. It should now comfort him that, whether the Lords are heeding him so far or not, the more able and perspicacious intellectuals of the ambiguously described 'Left' are revising their prejudices against the market and re-examining the reasons for its efficacy and increasing popularity that lie at the heart of the teachings of the no less ambiguously described 'new Right'. Although he finds the Government, which is at least trying, less culpable than the Opposition, which blindly ignores evidence of failure by the state, his philosophic position is liberal rather than conservative. A lordly Minister observed after a Harris speech: 'There is something about the *pur sang* of classical liberalism – very unlike the present incumbents – which is not my idea of conservatism but very much classical market liberalism ...'. The Harris speeches distil the essence of classical English (and Scottish) political economy which puts the general interest before special interests. Indeed, Lord Harris seems to have become the most consistent exponent of the general interest against some other peers who speak as 'experts' but for special interests – from mining to council housing and from opticians to (other) trade unionists; even the interests of the underdog – or the apparent underdog – from the unemployed to the disabled, are not always discussed by their lordships with requisite regard for the general interest.

Some liberal economists may differ from several of his judgements. The speeches nominate trade unions and management as the main culprits who have applied or tolerated restrictive practices in industry as the root cause of British economic decline. It could be argued that trade unions have introduced restrictive practices because the law gave them the power to enforce them and government thoughtlessly equipped them with complaisant employers in public service monopolies that could pass on the resulting costs to defenceless taypayers, especially in an inflationary environment. And managers tolerated restrictive practices because the economy was not sufficiently competitive to prevent them from passing the costs on to defenceless consumers. In both cases the ultimate culprit was government.

Not the least fruitful aspect of these speeches is their indications of the potential for influencing the upper chamber of the British Parliament by converting it from error. In his short five years Lord Harris has formed the view that the British economy requires not piecemeal reform but root-and-branch repeal of laws that have been outdated by technical advance but continue to hobble adaptation to change in supply and demand. To this end he has formed a non-party Repeal Group. Although repeal would presumably scare and alienate the peers even more than reform, his repealers have had some success, as in the argument on shop closing hours and on the opticians' monopoly. But so far the political and bureaucratic interests inside

[7]

government and the sectional interests in industry have prevailed against liberalisation in housing rents, minimum wages, licensing laws, coalmining and elsewhere for which he pleads eloquently. Marx, who emphasised the force of interests, has proved more prophetic than Keynes, who emphasised the influence of ideas.

Moreover, the political process in the British Parliament makes it necessary, or at least desirable, to disarm criticism by ritual genuflections that never question the motives of opponents:

> 'I do not doubt for one moment that many of the early pioneers and the modern inheritors of the trade union mantle were, and are, inspired by lofty idealism . . .'.

'Many' is an ambiguous word which conveys an impression of general public-spiritedness among British trade union leaders. The economics of public choice discounts differences in motives between people in bureaucratic institutions, whether governmental or private, and people in the market. Lord Harris quotes a Conservative Minister as saying: 'I rather like spending other people's money; it is one of the most enjoyable functions of a Minister's life'. His sad reaction is: 'I have come to accept that there is not much prospect of getting politicians to treat the taxpayer's money with the most especial respect it should deserve'.

On the whole, standards in the market are loftier than in bureaucracies because rogue elephants are discovered sooner through the sifting system of competition. In any event, people do good not because their motives are noble but because they are apt to go broke if they do not. Here, as elsewhere, Adam Smith the philosopher whom Lord Harris likes to quote saw more truth than Tawney or Titmuss or Tory patriarchs.

Yet, as Professor T. W. Hutchison has urged, John Stuart Mill was more prescient than both Marx and Keynes when he observed that ideas had to wait for 'circumstances' to 'conspire' in their favour. Lord Harris has had five years of economic proselytising. The Conservatives and perhaps the Social Democrats are listening; Labour and the Liberals mostly seem deaf; and the bishops are the most compassionately reactionary of all, with a culpable disdain for the opportunity costs of playing

God with other people's money. But Lord Harris is still young, as peers go, with at least two decades of reasoning and admonishing and exhorting to come in his 80s and into the 21st century. He deserves conspiring circumstance to come to his rescue sooner rather than later. Perhaps a monthly seminar in a Lords committee room on the elements of supply and demand, opportunity costs, elasticity, the difference between impact and incidence, the importance of price- as well as income-effects, and, not least, the economics of government and bureaucracy might help to save him time listening to sometimes over-simplified solutions to every 'problem'.

The Minister who distanced himself from Lord Harris's 'classical market liberalism' added that it had been 'an invaluable injection into the thinking of this Government and our national life . . .'. With rare exceptions, such as the late Lord Robbins, Lord Harris has been almost a lone wolf as an economic liberal in the Lords. He now has the prospect of reinforcement, not least by Professor Lord Bauer of Cambridge and the LSE, and he may receive aid from Lord Bruce-Gardyne, a Whig rather than a Tory, the non-economist Liberal Lord Grimond, who understands the market better than most British politicians in any Party, and the cross-bench trade unionist Lord Chapple, who once said, with a customary shaft of insight, 'In the end, it's the market or machine guns'.

If the Government is in earnest about deregulating an over-regulated economy, it could do worse (hardly better) than begin with the agenda of the Repeal Group which – in addition to wages councils, rent control, Shops Acts, licensing laws, and the Truck Acts – includes employment protection, equal opportunities, social benefits for strikers and the NCB monopoly of working British coal resources. Many items have not yet reached its list. There is no lack of tasks for the avid dismantlers of the modern mercantilism.

In the meantime, these speeches provide all who feel strongly enough about economic liberalism – a growing congregation extending to hitherto sceptics as well as true believers – with model texts on how to embark on the task of persuading reluctant transgressors.

January 1985   ARTHUR SELDON

The Author

RALPH HARRIS was born in 1924 and educated at Tottenham Grammar School and Queens' College, Cambridge. He was Lecturer in Political Economy at St Andrews University, 1949-56, and has been General Director of the Institute of Economic Affairs since 1957. He wrote (with Arthur Seldon) *Hire Purchase in a Free Society, Advertising in a Free Society, Choice in Welfare*, etc., for the IEA. His essay, 'In Place of Incomes Policy', was published in *Catch '76 . . .?* (Occasional Paper 'Special' (No. 47), 1976). His most recent works, written with Arthur Seldon, are *Pricing or Taxing?* (Hobart Paper No. 71, 1976), *Not from Benevolence . . .*(Hobart Paperback No. 10, 1977), and *Over-ruled on Welfare* (Hobart Paperback No. 13, 1979); he contributed the Epilogue, 'Can Confrontation be Avoided?', to *The Coming Confrontation* (Hobart Paperback No. 12, 1978); and his most recent IEA titles are *The End of Government . . .?* (Occasional Paper No. 58, 1980), and (with Arthur Seldon) *Shoppers' Choice* (Occasional Paper No. 68, 1983).

He is a Trustee of the Wincott Foundation and a member of the Political Economy Club, former President of the Mont Pélèrin Society, and a Council Member of the University of Buckingham.

Ralph Harris was created a Life Peer in July 1979 as Lord Harris of High Cross.

PART I:
Unions and Unemployment

---

1. A WELCOME FOR THE TEBBIT BILL

Debate on the Second Reading of the 1982 Employment Bill

IN ITS press advertising campaign against the Employment Bill, the TUC said that Mr Tebbit is 'trying to crush trade unions'. Like Lord Marsh, I can think of some trade union leaders who could do with a bit of crushing. But I want to explain why I think the TUC claim is so misguided by reference to German unions which have achieved so much more for their members without the privileges demanded with menaces by the TUC and their dwindling friends.

If this Bill were passed unchanged, British trade union leaders would still enjoy massive powers not available to their German counterparts. The proof is set forth in the Green Paper on immunities.[1] Thus in Germany the closed shop is illegal and membership of the 17 industrial unions ranges from above 90 per cent down to 10 per cent. Collective agreements are binding and trade unions can be sued like other responsible bodies for breach of contract. The rules of all but one of the 17 German unions require a 75 per cent vote in a secret ballot to approve industrial action. Finally, German public servants have no right to strike, and indeed for all unions political strikes and political affiliations are forbidden.

I believe the contrast with Germany is instructive because, since the beginning of this century, average British wages have fallen from almost double the German level to nearer half today. My argument is that the chief cause of our long relative economic decline has been the unique power of British trade unions to restrict flexibility and efficiency, to obstruct or sterilise invest-

---

[1] *The Consultative Document on Trade Union Immunities*, Cmnd. 8128, HMSO, January 1981.

ment, to discourage management in all its endeavours and so to retard economic progress. It is legendary that professional economists have wide disagreements. But I believe that most will accept that a necessary, if not a sufficient, condition for economic progress must be the continuous adaptation of working methods to match ceaseless changes in techniques, products, competition, comparative costs and consumer demand.

To go back to the TUC commercial last week, I thought its most inventive claim was that trade unions 'stand for the future'. Trade unions stand for the future like the Argentine junta stands for sweetness and light. It would be a closer approximation to the truth to say that British trade unions include the most backward-looking, nostalgic and reactionary bodies since the Society for the Preservation of Rural England.

It is sometimes thought that such museum pieces as the ASLEF train drivers, the printers, the dockers, the TV crews and even the miners are passing aberrations, and that they are exceptional in their obstruction to efficiency. But a truer observation, in my view, would be that British trade unions have historically too often stood for restrictionism. Their over-bearing legal powers have first magnified and then institutionalised the natural human resistance to change, which is one of the most common barriers to economic progress.

Examples of Luddism

For historical evidence, I will offer two episodes in the long catalogue of Luddism. The first goes back to 1897 when the new model trade union, the Amalgamated Society of Engineers, went on strike over the manning of machines – how many men to a machine was the issue. My witness is the Cambridge Professor of Economics, Alfred Marshall, who was known to be a warmer friend of trade unions and of the co-operative movement than he ever would have been of the employers. Not wishing to take sides publicly against the union, he poured out his frustrations in a private letter to the Master of Balliol, which included the following sentence:

'If the men should win and I were an engineering employer, I would sell my works for anything I could get and emigrate to America'.

[12]

He went on in a later letter to refer to trade union restrictions in the bricklayers' union; and on locomotives he noted: 'Three Glasgow men needed to do the work of one American'.

Marshall did not by any means exempt complacent management from his strictures, but he saw the strongest threat to what he called 'national wellbeing' as

'the dominance in some unions of the desire to "make work" and an increase in their power to do so'.

That was before 1906, when the Liberal Government was pressurised into conceding these large immunities in the teeth of strong opposition from Asquith and his legal colleagues in that Cabinet.

My second example of the arch conservatism of trade unions is drawn from the war. After 1939 it was discovered very quickly that the munitions industries could not work with the customary restrictions on entry, manning and demarcation. It was also found that for many jobs girls could be trained in a few months to replace time-served craftsmen who had been called-up. The official war history rather delicately describes this episode and mentions how even Ernie Bevin, formerly a trade union secretary and now war-time Minister of Labour, was unable to get agreement to what was called 'dilution' from his trade union colleagues without a cast-iron guarantee to revert to the *status quo ante* the moment the war was over. So it came about that, in 1942, Parliament turned aside from more pressing business to pass a full-blown statute, the Restoration of Pre-War Trade Practices Act. Its explicit purpose was to ensure that the efficient methods devised to win the war should not be available in helping to win the peace.

I do not doubt for one moment that many of the early pioneers and the modern inheritors of the trade union mantle were, and are, inspired by lofty idealism and voluntary action. It seems to me that the real error of many of their more political colleagues has been to seek higher wages through monopoly pressure and restrictionism, rather than through efficiency and expansion in marketable output. Their astonishing, if unintended, achievement has been simultaneously to depress British standards of living while inflating money wages and costs so as to cause an alternation between faster inflation and rising unemployment.

[13]

It has taken the deepest post-war recession to enable managements in the private sector to win support from their employees, often over the heads of the trade union leaders, for the shedding of decades of slack working habits. It seems to me that this beneficial process would be assisted and extended into the public sector if this Bill went further in relieving trade union leaders of their self-destructive weaponry.

2. LABOUR COSTS VERSUS JOBS

Debate on the Queen's Speech, following the
1983 General Election

IT IS a new experience for me to follow Lord Kaldor, with whom I have had some disagreements in the past. But on this occasion I think it might be best to respect the informal economists' protection society by not immediatetly following his speculations on Saatchi and Saatchi, George Orwell and sundry other matters, which I found difficult to follow. Rather, I would start by congratulating Lord Bauer on what I thought was a notable maiden contribution to our discussion. I thought his cogent criticism of the welfare state for robbing individuals of responsibility was by no means lacking in true concern and compassion, which is often interpreted in a different way by the Labour side of this House.

In a rather different mood, I enjoyed the typically combative performance of Lord Bruce of Donnington. When I am listening to him I always think that he is somebody I should like to have with me in a tight corner. But until he faces the right way I have decided that it would be better to keep out of tight corners. I can agree with him from the cross-benches on one matter: that the Queen's Speech is sadly lacking on the major issue of unemployment. Even if we allow, as I would, that the official statistics include a good deal of voluntary unemployment – as well as ignoring the black market – the lack of job prospects remains a dark shadow, especially over the lives of young people. But on this occasion Lord Bruce turned aside to offer some interesting reflections on past Tory failures. Some of his criticisms of the exchange rate might be seen with hindsight to have some justice, but he overlooked telling us what proposals he had in mind to

No, Minister!
RALPH HARRIS

1. The economy is still suffering the after-effects of the British disease caused by a combination of short-sighted trade unions and excessive government spending, taxation and regulation.

2. Trade unions have restricted production and standards of living whilst forcing-up money wages which caused the past alternation between rising inflation and higher unemployment.

3. So long as previous governments pursued full employment without full production, unions and management had no incentive to put their house in order.

4. Managements in local government, education and health services still lack the market disciplines that have compelled private enterprise since 1979 to begin shedding under-employed labour and other slack working habits.

5. The present 'mixed economy' is still half-way to full-blown collectivism with the present Government spending more than half of the national income, employing nearly one-third of the labour force and intervening extensively throughout the economy.

6. Since the Liberal Government of 1906 there has been a progressive shift from dispersed initiative in competitive markets towards increasing centralisation, bureaucracy and state power.

7. Most economic and social disorders spring not from malevolent design but from well-intended policies that go wrong, or from attempts by politicians to buy votes with promissory notes called election pledges.

8. Wages councils, the opticians' monopoly and rent control are examples of political distortions in market pricing that damage the supposed beneficiaries and should be repealed.

[Continued]

Occasional Paper 71 is published (price £1·80) by

 THE INSTITUTE OF ECONOMIC AFFAIRS
2 Lord North Street, Westminster
London SW1P 3LB   Telephone: 01-799 3745

9. The Plan for Coal raised unrealistic expectations and was bound to lead to bitterness; competition requires at least the repeal of the section of the 1946 Nationalisation Act that gave the NCB the exclusive power of 'working and getting' all coal in Great Britain.

10. The best route towards higher employment is the further reduction of trade union power, government spending, taxation and other political distortions of competitive markets.

11. 'Reflationists' assume monetary expansion will act as a stimulant where in the past it acted as a sedative that sapped the will to tackle root causes, became addictive and stoked up inflation.

12. If we wish to extend employment without more inflation, the rough rule-of-thumb is that wages and salaries should increase by less than the rise in prices, except where employers have difficulty recruiting enough labour.

———————————

IEA OCCASIONAL PAPERS in print

*Wincott Memorial Lectures

IEA PUBLICATIONS

Subscription Service

An annual subscription is the most convenient way to obtain our publications. Every title we produce in all our regular series will be sent to you immediately on publication and without further charge, representing a substantial saving.

Subscription rates*

Britain: £15·00 p.a. including postage.

£14·00 p.a. if paid by Banker's Order.

£10·00 p.a. teachers and students who pay *personally*.

Europe and South America: £20 or equivalent.

Other countries: Rates on application. In most countries subscriptions are handled by local agents.

*These rates are *not* available to companies or to institutions.

To: The Treasurer, Institute of Economic Affairs,
2 Lord North Street,
Westminster, London SW1P 3LB.

I should like to subscribe beginning....................................
I enclose a cheque/postal order for:

☐ £15·00

☐ Please send me a Banker's Order form

☐ Please send me an Invoice

☐ £10·00 [I am a teacher/student at............................]

Name...

Address..

....

Signed... Date..................

support his amendment calling for relevant measures to reduce unemployment.

In anticipation of this coy modesty, I have turned again, for what the Labour Party called 'New Hope', to their election manifesto. There we find two main lines of action against unemployment. The first is the promise of what they call 'a massive programme for expansion', with increased public spending on investment, social services and most other things they can think of. This is the plausible Keynesian panacea, of which we got a whiff from Lord Kaldor. It is the doctrine that I dutifully imbibed with my beer at Cambridge after the war and went on for some years trying very hard to believe.

The alluring theory was that increased monetary demand would draw idle resources into employment. Alas! Repeated experience showed that once the trade union highwaymen got wind of this extra money on the road, they perfected their 'stand and deliver' act, whereby the larger part of the extra money got diverted into higher wages. It is to this spectacular wages snatch over the 1960s and 1970s that I trace our record of accelerating inflation and rising unemployment. Indeed, the Labour Party manifesto actually acknowledged this very danger. It sought to fend off the risk of inflation with all that stuff about 'a national economic assessment' – that is to say, a pow-wow with the highwaymen – which was code language among the faithful for another incomes policy.

Like a fifth or sixth marriage, it represents the triumph of hope over experience. The last time Mr Healey walked up the aisle with the TUC it was in the name of the 'social contract'. The outcome was that, between 1974 and 1979, total national spending increased by 130 per cent over five years. But of that massive spending spree, less than 10 percentage points went to raise output, while 110 percentage points went to boost prices. The modest rise in output was not enough to stop unemployment more than doubling under Labour – from below 600,000 to approaching 1½ million.

If we turn to the Conservative Government, we find that the last Chancellor did not reduce demand but only the rate at which it increased. Thus, from 1979 to 1982, total spending still rose by 45 per cent over the three years. The result was that prices increased by 50 per cent and output fell by around 4 per cent, with unemployment again doubling – from 1½ million to 3 million.

From all this I deduce, by logic which I have not time fully to elaborate, that the Government's target for monetary growth of 7 to 11 per cent this year is perfectly consistent with declining inflation and increased output only so long as the additional spending is not absorbed by higher costs.

Causes of unemployment

We are therefore brought back to confront the central importance of labour costs as a cause not only of inflation but also of unemployment. I have some hope for at least silent agreement from the Labour benches because their manifesto promised further measures against unemployment, which rather gave away the whole trade union game. Thus, in addition to expanding demand, Labour promised a second line of action in the form of what it specifically called 'employment subsidies'. These were to be given to firms which avoided redundancies or created new jobs. But why subsidise wages if they are not already too high? Here was a frank admission that labour costs are above the market value of labour's contribution to output and are therefore at least one cause of unemployment.

This truth is illuminated by OECD figures which show that by 1981 labour costs in Britain had grown to absorb over 80 per cent of GNP, compared with around 70 per cent in France, Germany and Japan. Precisely the same trend is revealed by other indications of declining long-run profitability in British industry. Thus, if we exclude North Sea oil, we find that the average real rate of return on capital in Britain fell from above 10 per cent in the 1960s to 5 per cent in 1979 and 2 or 3 per cent more recently. We really cannot escape the conclusion that a major domestic cause of avoidably high unemployment is the rise in labour costs per unit of output and the resulting decline in profitability. Such a shift in rewards must reduce the incentive to employ more people. At the same time, it reduces the funds available for investment which would create jobs directly in new buildings and plant, or indirectly by improving efficiency and sales in competition with foreign suppliers.

We all say, and endlessly repeat, that we deplore the economic

[16]

and social consequences of unemployment. But suppose we cared above all else for bringing lasting jobs to those who are genuinely seeking work, would we really go into the Lobbies again to preserve the Wages Councils which we know, at the margin, price young people out of the market? Suppose we cared less for maintaining outdated political prejudices, might we not think of new ways to encourage employment, mobility, investment and, if I dare say it, entrepreneurship? What about such measures as repealing stamp duties, reducing the tax on capital transfers and stock options, or encouraging portable pensions? Not least, what about ending the taxation of low incomes, which now reduces take-home pay to little, if anything, above the value of social benefits?

As a gesture, for my part I would overcome my deep doubts and distrust about further government intervention and even agree to some new programme of public spending, if only it could be shown not to make things worse by raising taxes and other costs elsewhere so as to damage existing employment.

My concluding thought is that an agenda for radical reform to reduce unemployment would range far wider than the measures outlined in the Queen's Speech. Certainly, it would include action on nationalised industries, trade unions and local authority spending – for the reasons so splendidly developed by Lord Boyd-Carpenter and Lord Marsh. But it would extend to long-overdue measures to reduce government spending and taxes – especially for misdirected welfare – which was so powerfully exposed by Lord Bauer from the Government benches.

3. WHEN LEN MURRAY WAS ALMOST RIGHT

Debate on a motion by Lord Wilson of Rievaulx (formerly Mr Harold Wilson) calling attention to high unemployment

I LISTENED with close attention to the speech of Lord Wilson of Rievaulx and thought I detected just a note of conflict between the fun he made of the low level of the exchange rate and the approach of his former economic adviser, Lord Kaldor, who made rather heavier work of the earlier rise in the exchange rate. But I do not doubt for a moment that Lord Wilson would be equal to providing a perfectly convincing reconciliation of this apparent disharmony.

I want briefly to join issue from the cross-benches with three claims that are most commonly heard from Labour speakers. The first concerns the magnitude of unemployment; the second is its true nature and cause; and the third, following Lord Thorneycroft, is what might be called non-solutions.

First, on magnitude, the challenge that confronts us is stern enough without rejoicing in exaggerated talk about 4 million, 4½ million or 5 million unemployed. Even the official figure, which is stuck around 3 million, conceals to some degree the active nature of the labour market, with a turnover every year of some 7 million changes of jobs. It also magnifies the jobless total, at least to the extent of the black economy, which some estimates have pitched as high as 1·4 million people. We may deplore the extent to which otherwise law-abiding citizens feel themselves driven into the underground economy, but it is instructive to ponder for one moment the reason. There cannot be much doubt that it is because the black economy comes closest to the free market, which was mocked by Lady Seear, where the cost of employing somebody is not inflated by taxes, closed shops, re-strictive practices, employment protection, equal opportunities, equal pay and all the rest.

This modest insight emphasises that the demand for labour depends chiefly upon its price. It seems to me not to require a grasp of higher economic theory to know that, other things being equal, the higher the cost of employing someone, the fewer will be the number of people likely to be employed. Otherwise, why has everyone joined in condemning the National Insurance Surcharge as a tax on jobs? Why did Labour's 1983 General Election manifesto call quite explicitly for employment subsidies, unless it was thought that the cost of employing people stood too high for their own good?

I have today a more telling witness to this truth in Mr Len Murray who, at a special conference in February to discuss the reduction of the working week, explicitly warned: 'There is a trade-off here. It is a trade-off between incomes and jobs'.

Even in this burst of candour the General Secretary of the TUC was not exactly accurate. Except in the black economy, the trade-off is not between incomes and jobs but between total labour cost and jobs. That is a very important distinction. The cost of employing a worker in the regular economy is not equal to the worker's take-home pay – as in the black economy – but nearer twice as much. The reason is that the employer faces, on top of wages, an on-cost of 30 or 40 per cent for National Insurance, pensions, employment protection, health and safety, and all the rest. On the other hand, the worker receives his wages only after deductions which can also amount, similarly, to 30 or 40 per cent of the wage paid by his employer. Governments have created a kind of topsy-turvy world which perversely combines high labour costs to employers with take-home pay often not much above social security benefits.

I am therefore led to take issue with those critics who blame unemployment and every other ill to which the economy is heir on the cruel operation of unchecked market forces unleashed by higher capitalism. Our famous mixed economy is well on the way to being a halfway house to full-blown collectivism. Even the present administration is spending more than half the national income and is employing nearly one-third of the entire labour force. In addition, it intervenes extensively throughout the whole economy with a confused mixture of subsidies and taxes – to say nothing of controls over all rents and the pay of more than 10 per cent of the labour force locked into Wages Councils. The resulting mess of political potage is not only an over-governed society but an inflexible, sclerotic economy that is slow to adjust output and jobs to new opportunities.

An end to phoney full employment

I come to my third issue of whether still more government is the cure or the chief cause of our economic malady. If we look back 20 years to the days when Lord Wilson was cheerfully lighting his pipe by the white heat of a technological revolution, we might recall all the well-intentioned but ill-fated policies to protect jobs and pick winners. Out of natural delicacy I will refrain from dwelling on the National Plan, which mocked nature by passing from teething troubles in 1965 to death rattles in 1966 without the customary interval of hopeful life. But what about all the nonsense of regional policy, indiscriminate subsidies, selective employment tax, bale-outs by courtesy of the

[19]

Industrial Reorganisation Corporation or the National Enterprise Board when the embrace of the state was often the prelude to the kiss of death? Those were the years when foreign observers diagnosed the 'British disease' and when more homespun talk against 'de-industrialisation' did not prevent jobs in manufacturing falling from 8·5 million in 1966 to little more than 7 million in 1979.

Looking forward in this debate, I hope Labour speakers will agree that there is not much scope here for self-righteous indignation over what is in my view the present unnecessarily high level of unemployment inflicted unintentionally by governments. In retrospect we can see that the seeds of our present troubles were sown in the years of phoney full employment without full efficiency. They were the years when trade unions insisted on two men doing the job of one man; when employers acquiesced in over-manning and opted for a quiet life even though their profits were declining; when governments of both Parties accommodated ever-rising costs by inflationary finance. Yet through those years – in the 1960s and 1970s – the trend towards rising unemployment was still visible. Throughout those dream decades of relative economic decline, what was most lacking was any effective penalty for the economic failure of unions and managements to put their ramshackle house in some kind of order.

It seems to me little surprise that the present Government is not basking in universal acclaim. It has been the first government since the war to make a start with restoring discipline, by phasing out the soft – and, I may say, 'wet' – option of cost-plus inflation. We should not wish it to contract out of the continuing struggle for higher employment through increased efficiency by returning to the discredited expedient of still higher government spending suggested by other speakers.

As we see from the National Union of Mineworkers, the National Union of Railwaymen, the National Union of Teachers and others, irresponsible union leaders are still lying in wait – ready to hi-jack any increase in monetary demand for unearned wage increases rather than for increased production or investment. If we wish to make room for more employment, the rough rule of thumb is that wages and salaries should increase by *less* than the rise in prices, except where employers have difficulty recruiting sufficient labour. That is what happens in many of the countries with which our industries and products have to compete. I say again to the Government that wage restraint along these lines would be far easier if they would re-apply their minds to ways of reducing government expenditure so as to make possible a continuing prospect of reduced taxes on low incomes.

Postscript by Lord Gowrie, answering for the Government

'. . . I was absolutely fascinated by that part of the debate when Lord Bottomley spoke and then Lord Harris of High Cross. There is simply no meeting of minds whatsoever. If Lord Bottomley reads the speech of Lord Harris, he will learn something – I would say to his advantage. If Lord Harris reads the speech of Lord Bottomley, he will see just how far he has still got to go in this economy in order to get people round to slightly nearer his point of view. When I listen to Lord Harris of High Cross, I always feel like a rather over-weight, middle-aged man – which is not, perhaps, too inaccurate a description – in the company of a seasoned jogger. There is something about the pur sang of classic liberalism – very unlike the present incumbents – which is not my idea of conservatism but very much classic market liberalism . . . which has been an invaluable injection into the thinking of this Government and our national life. . . .'

4. THE BRITISH DISEASE

Debate on a motion by Lord Cledwyn of Penrhos calling attention to the need to stimulate industrial growth

I HOPE it might be of service if I try to fill in something of the missing background of post-war economic difficulties, going back well before 1979, if we are to make any kind of judgement on recent developments. For example, have any of us forgotten all the endless agonising in the 1960s and 1970s over the British disease? Does Lord Cledwyn not recall all the talk of the economic league tables which showed our progressive decline from among the leaders to a straggling laggard in real income per head of developed nations?

I doubt if anyone in the House so easily remembers the post-war Anglo-American Council of Productivity which brought together the TUC and the Federation of British Industries in a rare search for ways of achieving greater efficiency. In 1953 it published a report with the hopeful title, *We Too Can Prosper*, which makes instructive reading some 30 years later. The author, Mr Graham Hutton, is a lifelong friend of mine and I recently read again with special care that he attributed the better performance of United States industry chiefly to their more intensive use of modern machines through the greater flexibility and mobility of labour. In contrast, Mr Hutton referred to the strong Luddite tradition of British trade unions which, allied to weak management, had given rise to what he then explicitly called 'concealed unemployment'. In my view, it has been, above all, the failure of managements to tackle restrictive practices in industry that explains Britain's long relative economic decline.

Of course, politicians have made endless speeches about productivity. The Conservative Party invented the National Economic Development Council, and the Labour Party conjured up national plans without number – and largely without effect. Both parties multiplied subsidies; at one time for capital investment, and then for the employment of labour. But I would argue that no sustained progress was made until after 1979.

If we go back to 1964, an American consultant, William Allen, hit the headlines in *The Sunday Times* with an article asking: 'Is Britain a half-time country, getting half pay for half work under half-hearted management?' His bleak answer gave countless examples from many differing industries where it took two or three British workers to produce as much as one in other countries, often with similar plant.

Two years after William Allen's article there was a debate in the House of Lords (May 1966) when Lord Byers from the Liberal benches opened a discussion on the need to increase efficiency. In that debate he estimated that between 10 and 20 per cent of the working population was under-employed. In the same debate, Lord Shawcross claimed that there was 'concealed under-employment of at least 2 million men and women', and he went on to argue that they would be available in expansionary times for redeployment in other industries and services.

If all this is even approximately true of that period, we are

[22]

bound to ask why managements and unions failed to grasp the nettle of slack working habits. It is a non-political revelation that these restrictive practices were deeply embedded in industry and indeed go back more than half a century to the birth of British trade unionism. When we look even in recent years to examples in printing, docks, railways, shipbuilding, most recently in the car industry, we find that where managements do tackle restrictive practices or overmanning they are in for costly battles which, in some cases, can set a term to the existence of their companies.

Soft option of inflation

Against the confrontation that would have been involved to tackle these problems, it was so much easier for the CBI and the TUC to get together at their cosy meetings and to press government to stimulate demand for inefficient labour in the sacred name of Keynesian full employment policies. That is the nub of my criticism of that period. I believe it has been the major cause of Britain's record inflation, and I think it is also the explanation of Britain's poor record of growth and the consequent industrial decline.

The lesson ignored by today's self-styled 'reflationists' is that monetary expansion – though again and again intended as a stimulant to employment and growth – simply acted as a sedative that sapped the will to tackle the root causes of our poor industrial performance. Even worse, these political pep pills became addictive, so that increasing doses yielded a diminishing effect on employment and output, with worsening side-effects on inflation. As Hayek has pointed out, more and more jobs became dependent not only on the continuation of inflation but on its acceleration. That helps to explain why the Labour Government's success after 1974 in getting inflation down pushed unemployment up – under a Labour Government – very close to 1½ million.

It is true that the real wages of British workers rose more slowly than elsewhere, but they still rose faster than flagging output. Positive proof, from a great many conflicting statistics, is shown by the decline in the real rate of return on capital from an average of 10 per cent in the 1960s to below 5 per cent in 1979, which was an ill omen of higher unemployment still to come.

[23]

The crime with which this Government is charged is simply that it has refused to accommodate the higher inflation that would have been necessary to keep workers in over-priced jobs. The Government is not guilty of reducing or deflating demand, but only of allowing it to grow more slowly to bring inflation down from above 20 per cent to below 5 per cent. In the process, the concealed unemployment of the 1950s and 1960s has come out into the open and onto the register. I agree that it is nothing less than tragedy that this long overdue corrective for the en-feebling British disease coincided with a record world recession on top of a structural shift of industry into new products and new sources of supply for older products.

I conclude with the thought that there is a silver lining to the heavy clouds of unemployment. It is that in many sectors of industry there has been a dramatic rise in productivity since management and trade unions found they could not take the soft option of inflating their costs and prices. As I have said before, Mrs Thatcher is like the wife who has hidden the gin – and that is not popular, especially among old soaks who are by no means confined to the Labour benches. I believe it gives us the best chance since the war to expand our production and employment as the world recovers from a recession, which has been little more than a return to earth after the prolonged illusory joy-ride of international monetary inflation.

PART II:
Cases for Repeal

5. Towards Limited Government

Debate on a motion by Lord Renton calling attention to the volume of legislation and the desirability of repealing outdated or unnecessary statutes

PERHAPS I should start, almost as a maiden speaker, by asking for the indulgence of other speakers who bring such legal distinction to our discussion of the quantity and quality of legislation. As a mere economist, my approach will be somewhat more down-to-earth – although others may wish to describe it rather differently. As Lord Elwyn-Jones partly implied, much of the indiscriminate multiplication of statutes has aimed to improve our economic and social welfare, yet it has conspicuously failed to usher in the promised millennium.

In economics we have a serviceable law of diminishing marginal utility. It is the neglected foundation of much economic analysis and tells us that increasing supplies tends to decrease the additional value or satisfaction we derive from any line of consumption. So it has proved with legislation; the growing volume has led to diminishing utility. There is no dispute among us about the long-run tendency for the quantity of legislation to increase. With 3,100 general public Acts in force, plus 13,000 general statutory instruments, it is surely not inappropriate to talk of an over-governed nation sinking in a morass of regulation and control – much of it wholly incomprehensible to the layman and apparently even to Lord Denning.[1]

I am not a wild anarchist. I regard law as the indispensable buttress of all our prized freedoms, but we can have too much

---

[1] Earlier in the debate Lord Denning, for 20 years (1962-82) Master of the Rolls, had condemned 'our statutes [as] still appalling in their complexity', and referred to Section 17 of the Employment Act 1980 as 'the most tortuous section I have ever read. It defies understanding'.

even of so good a thing. We have carried the necessary ordinances to the point of inordinacy. It is an example of the same undisciplined tendency to excess which Sir William Rees-Mogg has blamed for monetary inflation. For me the lesson is that we urgently need to restore limits to both the activity and ambitions of modern government.

I believe the best guide for the reforming efforts of lawyers, economists and others may be found in the seminal trilogy by Professor Hayek entitled *Law, Legislation and Liberty*. Even if time allowed, I am not qualified to do justice to Professor Hayek's grand thesis. But I found helpful his distinction between law, as the evolution of general rules of just conduct, and legislation, as the often arbitrary commands of governments vested with temporary authority to impose their will or even their whims. Thus legislation is often linked only rhetorically with any universal, permanent principles of justice, of equity, or indeed of law itself in its original meaning.

Special-interest groups

Hayek is not the only economic philosopher to diagnose legislative incontinence as the occupational hazard of politicians in a democracy. The economic analysis of politics starts from the commonplace observation that politicians are not wholly disinterested in gaining votes. Of course they have long-term ideals, and I understand that some even have principles. But such intellectual baggage tends to get mislaid or left behind in their natural haste to win a majority. The simplest way to amass votes at one time was for politicians to buy them. But since open corruption was made illegal – and was anyway expensive – the next best thing was to buy votes with promissory notes, politely referred to as election pledges.

Instead of bidding for individual votes, parties have come to seek wholesale support from large or powerful groups such as trade unionists, farmers, old-age pensioners, tenants, owner-occupiers, and other significant minorities. The method is to pass laws conferring privileges or immunities on sufficient special-interest groups to build up a winning coalition of votes.

One reason why politicians are vulnerable to pressure from lobbies of sectional interests is that democratic governments are thought to be omnipotent. They have unlimited powers to pass laws to remedy every passing grievance, real or imagined. As we now see, when the ruling party withholds its favours, an irresponsible Opposition stands ready to promise to oblige after the next election. Thus, unlimited government has unchained insupportable demands from the populace and has brought nominally all-powerful government to the brink of impotence.

By a different route from that taken by Lord Hailsham in his remarkable Dimbleby Lecture, I have come to follow Professor Hayek in favouring a written constitution. Its aim would be to entrench limited government – perhaps even by specifying limits on the discretion of politicians to spend, to tax, to expropriate, and maybe even to discriminate in favour of sectional interests.

All that is for discussion and for the future. Meanwhile, I should like from the cross-benches to commend the efforts of the non-party Repeal Group, which encouraged Lord Renton to bring this debate before us. The Repeal Group offers a modest prospect of relief from excessive legislation by seeking the outright repeal of unnecessary or restrictive statutes. As Lord Renton has said, we have made a start with Lady Trumpington's Bill to end the Shops Acts. After the Recess, there will be a chance to debate the Second Readings of the Rent (Abolition of Control) Bill introduced by Lord Vaizey, and the Truck Acts (Repeal) Bill, which I introduced recently. Like Ko-Ko in *The Mikado*, we 'have a list of society offenders that never would be missed', and we would welcome suggestions for statutes to be added to our worthy candidates for repeal.

6. STATUTORY MINIMUM WAGES

*Debate on the Second Reading of the Wages Councils
(Abolition) Bill moved by the late Lord Spens*

I CONGRATULATE Lord Spens for his perseverance in moving from asking polite questions about Wages Councils to proposing their outright abolition. In this he has the support of the informal group known as the Repeal Group, whose efforts I referred to when Lady Trumpington moved her Bill to repeal the Shops Acts in February. I am delighted to follow Lord Roberthall and

[27]

hope to demonstrate that economists are not obliged to disagree. I urge him to keep on raising his voice in the Alliance, because he may help to lead the Lady Seear back into the paths of true liberalism.

The case for this Bill is a good deal stronger than that for the Shops Bill, to which we recently gave an unopposed Second Reading. Wages Councils had their origins in 1909, when four Trade Boards were set up to fix minimum wages in the sweated trades of tailoring, lace-, box- and chain-making. The Act was extended in 1918, and the Boards were renamed Wages Councils in 1945. Since 1938 the tally of workers covered has increased from 1½ million to 2¾ million.

A number of speakers have raised the question that what was fitting in 1909 – when workers lacked the bargaining power that comes from education, from knowledge, from employment exchanges, from easier mobility and from generous social benefits – bears no relation whatsoever to the conditions of the 1980s. Lady Seear might ponder the transformation in conditions of domestic servants before telling us these stories about the likelihood of workers being greatly exploited in the absence of minimum wages.

It seems to me that what started as benevolent welfare policy has come to exert a malevolent economic effect. It has done so at a time when low pay has much less to do with poverty because the low-paid are preponderantly young people or women who live in households with two or more earners. What is worse, from prescribing bare minimum wages which the least efficient employer was compelled to pay, Wages Councils have come to set what they regard as 'reasonable' wages, especially for young people, at levels that even the most profitable firms find it difficult to improve upon.

The report *Priced Out* by the National Federation of Self-Employed and Small Businesses shows that during the 1970s the dubious 'independents' and employers' representatives on these Councils did not prevent the more single-minded trade union representatives from pushing up wages much faster than inflation. The figures show that over this decade the six largest Councils increased adult wages 4-fold and juvenile wages 4½-fold, compared with a 3-fold rise in prices. At the same time, in retailing the age at which the adult wage was paid has been lowered from 21 to 19. So that whereas, 10 years ago, a school-leaver would start at a little over half the adult wage, he must now be paid 60 per cent, and by the age of 18 he must be paid 85 per cent of the wage of an adult with perhaps a lifetime of working experience.

The Wages Orders issued by the Councils are often of the most baffling complexity. They deal with holidays, hours, regions, meal and rest breaks and unsocial hours, and they prescribe different rates of pay at varying times. An LSE study in 1980 identified in one Wages Council that 166 minimum rates were prescribed. The personnel director of a leading retail chain has told me that he could not be sure of understanding the annual changes even when he had expert legal advice at his elbow. Nor are wage costs the end of the matter. At least 30 per cent must be added for national insurance and other employment expenses, without allowing for what are called compliance costs and for such benefits in kind as staff buying discounts and meals, which are totally ignored by the jolly quango men on these Wages Councils.

Effect on employment

There can be no doubt that the escalation of total wage costs has reduced employment opportunities. The foundation of all economic analysis is nothing more arcane than that prices affect quantities. If wages are increased, other things being equal, the demand for workers will be reduced at the margin. All the empirical evidence on the operation of minimum wages, particularly in the United States over a very long period, shows that they cause unemployment especially among the most vulnerable. Two leading black American economists, Professors Thomas Sowell and Walter Williams, have recently shown that when the cost of employing people is artificially raised under the Federal minimum wage law, the resulting unemployment is concentrated on the young, unskilled, inexperienced, female and, even more severely, on the ethnic minorities.

Nowhere – except perhaps in rent control – has well-intentioned policy produced more perversely damaging results than in raising wages without regard for market realities. Thus in Britain the pace has been set by the Low Pay Unit, which would today be more accurately branded the 'No Pay Unit'. Why could they not learn from the evil experience of South Africa, where minimum wages were deliberately supported by white trade unionists to reduce the job opportunities of unskilled black workers by pricing them out of the labour market?

It is no use opponents of this Bill taking refuge behind their undoubted good intentions. In economics – as in much well-meant private conduct – good intentions are no guarantee of good results. In Britain the bleak road to high unemployment has been paved with good intentions. Indeed, all our most grievous economic and social disorders have been caused not by malevolent design but by the amiable confusions of mis-named 'do-gooders', who undoubtedly meant well but who have inadvertently caused much of the havoc that we see around us.

I hope we shall avoid verbal competition in compassion. There is no important difference between us in all parts of the House on the principle of a minimum income. But whether that is provided through supplementary benefits or, as I would prefer, through a reverse income tax, it is the province of social policy and should not be attempted by manipulating prices, such as wages, rents or interest rates, which must lead to costly distortions throughout the economy. Whatever the sceptics may say, we know that wages can be too high for the good of employment. That is why Labour and Conservative governments have been driven to multiply job subsidies – especially for the young – simply to undo the damage of trade union wage-push. It is also why some workers have voluntarily settled for wage standstills or even for wage reductions to save jobs – an option that is rendered illegal by the Government's stubborn enforcement of the Act which we are now seeking to repeal.

I urge all who care more for reducing unemployment than for preserving their emotional purity to join in supporting this Bill, if necessary through the Lobby.[1]

[1] As a result of Labour and Liberal opposition and Conservative abstentions, the Bill was defeated by 42 votes to 25.

7. The Opticians' Monopoly

*Debate on the Second Reading of the Opticians Act 1958
(Amendment) Bill moved by Lord Rugby*

I CONGRATULATE Lord Rugby on his persistence and perseverance over a number of years in opposing the opticians' monopoly in selling reading glasses. The Repeal Group has encouraged him to bring this Bill forward and I personally hope that he is ready to carry the issue to a Division if that looks like being necessary to jolt the Government into taking some action in place of their repeated words of concern.

Others have exposed the questionable, if not false, medical arguments that buttress the present scheme which requires 7 million people buying glasses each year to shop at a registered optician for what are grandly called their 'optical appliances'. I want to develop a more general argument. The essence of my complaint against Section 21 of the 1958 Opticians Act is that it confuses the roles of the professional and the tradesman in a single person and gives that person power to raise his income by keeping up the price of what he sells.

The consequent abuse of collusion among opticians was predicted over 200 years ago by Adam Smith in *The Wealth of Nations* from which I will offer one of my favourite quotations:

'People of the same trade seldom meet together even for merriment and diversion, but the conversation ends in a conspiracy against the public, or in some contrivance to raise prices'.

In this, a profession is not wholly different from a trade union which naturally endeavours to raise the income of its members by restricting competition from alternative suppliers who could do the job equally well. Lord Richardson[1] took the view that anyone concerned with the profession of medicine or its ancillary activities is somehow above concern for his income. I beg leave to doubt that – and I could bring many friends from the medical profession, at any rate in private, to my side against him.

No-one denies that opticians perform valuable services and that may include diagnosing eye diseases which call for treatment. For this purpose opticians receive due training, as do electricians. But we are not required to hire an electrician when we

[1] A former President of the General Medical Council on the cross-benches.

[31]

want to change a light bulb or to mend a fuse. Yet most people who, as Lord Rugby said, wear glasses for simple magnification are now legally compelled to go through a full medical examination each time they want stronger spectacles and are then compelled to buy those spectacles from a registered optician. It was likened by Lord Winstanley,[1] in an earlier contribution, to requiring a medical examination before allowing anyone to buy a walking stick. He did not add that it would also be like giving doctors a monopoly of selling walking sticks, which we may be sure would then come in more ornate varieties at suitably fancy prices.

If we turn to another useful profession, it is true that regular dental examination can spot tooth decay. But we would not think of making everyone buying a toothbrush go to the dentist and buy their toothbrush only after submitting to a full inspection of teeth. Periodic check-ups with dentists or with opticians are a matter of prudence. May I suggest to Lord Hunter[2] that the proper role of compulsion in optics is in school examination of eyes, especially for squints which I gather are best corrected at an early age.

Special pleading

Despite what we have heard, it remains true that among the fears that are played upon by the apologists for the opticians' cartel is the old wives' tale that wearing the wrong glasses can damage your eyes. We are now told that it can no more damage your eyes than listening to pop music might damage your ears. I think the House ought to recognise that the opticians' union is running one of the most blatant, government-protected closed shops. Of course, it dresses up its special pleading in a professional white coat. The game was rather given away in an earlier code of practice by the now-defunct British Optical Association, which regretted that for over 300 years opticians had practised in shop premises and went on to urge them to get away from the shop atmosphere and above all advised:

'No prices should be exhibited, otherwise the optician can hardly

---

[1] A practising GP on the Liberal benches.
[2] A former Professor of Pharmacology on the cross-benches.

escape from the accusation that he is a salesman rather than a professional man'.

Difficult though it may be for some of the earlier speakers to accept, I believe that there is no hard and fast dividing line between a profession and skilled trade – except perhaps the accent of the practitioners. There is certainly no justification for questioning the restrictive practices of ASLEF and SOGAT whilst viewing the professional restrictive practices that we are here concerned with through the rose-tinted spectacles conveniently provided free by the Association of Optical Practitioners. I would venture to say that anyone who cannot see through this optical illusion needs more than his eyes examined.

Accordingly, I commend this Bill[1] and would leave with you the magisterial words of a leading article in *The British Medical Journal* of 13 December 1980:

'Deletion of the monopoly clause from the Act . . . will be hotly contested by opticians. Yet what harm would result? As in other countries where there are no statutory restrictions, the mass of the public would continue to have their eyes tested by opticians or eye doctors, and the simple purchase of glasses over the counter would be confined to the normal-sighted over-50s who simply need reading help'.

8. No Truck with Cash

Debate on the Second Reading of the Truck Acts (Repeal) Bill moved by Lord Harris of High Cross

IN BRINGING this Bill before you from the cross-benches, I have been encouraged by the non-party Repeal Group. It has three purposes: first, by the simple device of repeal to slim the statute book which has become grossly inflated until, like a fat man, we can no longer see where we are putting our feet. Secondly, we wish to reinforce Her Majesty's Government on the urgent need to set limits to endless talk and to speed action. Our third substantive aim is to remove an obsolete barrier to spreading payment of wages by a variety of more modern, economic and safe methods than carting £1,000 million of notes and coin around the country every pay-day.

[1] Lord Rugby withdrew his Bill, but the opticians' monopoly was repealed by the Health and Social Security Act 1984.

The origins of the Truck Acts take us back to a vanished world peopled by such ghosts as the 'bagmen', 'petty foggers', 'butties' and other middlemen who paid workers in goods or in 'tommy tickets' that could be exchanged only at the company store or 'truck shop' which belonged to their employer. 'Truck' apparently comes from the French word, 'troc', meaning barter, and it sometimes served a useful purpose in earlier centuries when people lived and worked in remote districts away from towns or markets. But it was open to the obvious abuse of any monopoly and became the target of public policy as early as 1411 when a local ordinance required Colchester weavers to be paid in gold and silver rather than in merchandise or victuals.

The Truck Acts (Repeal) Bill would decently bury the carcases of five outdated laws. The 1831 Act in its time replaced no fewer than 19 statutes by a wide prohibition against contracts for artificers' wages being specified in other than 'current coin of the realm'. Its 27 clauses applied to a dozen specified trades and excluded agriculture and domestic service. The 1887 Truck Amendment Act extended protection to all manual workers covered by the Employer and Workmen Act of 1875. The 1896 Act strengthened protection against deductions from wages. In 1940 a further Act was necessary to protect employers against some of the resulting anomalies – for example, where meals were served at work. Finally, the 1960 Payment of Wages Act permitted payment in postal orders, money orders, cheques or direct bank credit in place of cash. But it allowed these alternatives to cash subject to three conditions: first, that the employee agrees in writing to forgo cash; secondly, that he can withdraw that agreement at four weeks' notice; and thirdly, that the employer provides a full statement of gross wages and deductions.

Reflecting on the amendment in the name of Lord Rochester, I imagine that at some Liberal seminar on the theme of 'Forward from 1831' my legal outline might be puffed up to sound a progressive and satisfying development. The reality is less flattering to our Parliamentary forbears. As was made clear by the American scholar Professor George W. Hilton in his standard work entitled *The Truck System*,[1] most of these laws were out of date before they were enacted. Thus the practice of truck has been extinct for more than a century and the only patchy

[1] Published by Heffer, Cambridge, 1960.

remnants of any value in this legal rag-bag relate to deductions from wages.

It is central to my case that deductions from wages could be far better dealt with under the quite separate Contract of Employment Act of 1963 and the Employment Protection (Consolidation) Act of 1978. In the contemporary world of written contracts of employment, it should be straightforward to protect everyone, not only manual workers, against unauthorised deductions by extending the right of appeal to industrial tribunals. In this way we can satisfy what matters in our obligations under the International Labour Organisation and the European Social Charter.

Central fallacy

The Truck Acts are not merely an historical curiosity and therefore apparently beloved by the Liberal Party as the museum for lost causes. The law as it now stands has become a positive nuisance. It is like the decayed remnants of some long-dead corpse that has been resurrected to serve a purpose wholly different from its original intention. As a non-lawyer, I hope to make clear what is the central fallacy in the modern interpretation of the Truck Acts and the resulting error, as I see it, that was embodied in the Payment of Wages Act 1960.

The plain purpose of the historical campaign against truck was to ensure that workers were not paid in goods. The aim was never to guarantee that they were paid in some specified form of money. Indeed, the 1831 Act said that the contract was to be made in cash. Of course, in the 19th century coins were the standard medium of exchange, just as today cheques, bank cards, Giro, and direct debit are the predominant means of payment. Even so, Section 8 of the 1831 Act provided that workers *could* be paid by a cheque drawn on the Bank of England or on any other note-issuing bank within 15 miles of their place of work.

This neglected provision completely explodes the case of those TUC Luddites who now want to go on discussing and negotiating for ever to delay action on the switch from cash to credit transfer. The key safeguard of the 1831 Act and subsequent Acts was not cash in the form of coins, but generalised purchasing power in place of payment in unwanted goods. It was only the accident of the 1844 monopoly of the Bank of England over the issuing of notes that invalidated Section 8 and made the Payment of Wages Act 1960 necessary. Yet this latest Act now works to slow down the development of those very modern means of payment through the banks that were its original justification.

The chief obstacle to progress in various forms of credit transfer is the unjustified requirement that, not only must every worker give written permission to be paid by cheque, but that he can at any time change his mind and at four weeks' notice insist on cash. Thus, we find that a complex system of law evolved over 400 years to prevent a forgotten abuse can, 150 years later, be brandished to obstruct developments beneficial to workers no less than to the economy and to society.

Is it any wonder that we lag so far behind America and Europe, with 13 million British earners still paid by the week and over 10 million paid in dangerous, clumsy and inefficient cash? The Central Policy Review Staff in 1981 doubted whether the Truck Acts were high on the list of obstacles to further progress. With rather more direct knowledge, employers have called for repeal of the Truck Acts as a barrier to modern methods of payment. Among the leading supporters of this Bill I am pleased to cite the Confederation of British Industry, the National Federation of Building Trades Employers, the Engineering Employers Federation, and the Federation of Civil Engineering Contractors. No less impressive, the Institute of Personnel Management has supported repeal of the Truck Acts as an overdue step towards obliterating the increasingly meaningless distinction between wages and salaries, as between workers and staff.

More than 20 years ago the Karmel Committee[1] urged repeal. Since then the banks have improved their services, including more flexible opening hours and wider access to cash dispensers. Further developments are already on the way. I believe that few initiatives would give stronger encouragement to the rapid extension of an efficient, modern banking network serving the entire population than the repeal of these backward-looking statutes. I beg to move that the Bill be now read a second time.

*　　　　*　　　　*

Postscript: Reply to the Debate
I should like to thank all the speakers who have taken part in this admirable, brief debate. I do not think a good case has been

[1] *Report of the Committee on the Truck Acts*, HMSO, 1961.

made out for the amendment,[1] and I do not think the Lord Rochester gave any reference to the merits of the present truck legislation. Nothing I have heard suggests the least difficulty about giving the Bill a Second Reading and continuing at Committee stage the discussions about the single issue of deductions. In view of the Minister's most amiable advice on these matters, and also in view of his splendid attack on the pretext of the Liberal amendment, I want to offer him a warning, if it is not impertinent. My warning is that he may find his advisers are making rather heavy weather of the international conventions and charters. Having poured over these stupefyingly mundane documents in recent weeks, I find them to be mountains of bureaucratic pomposity, signifying very little indeed.

For example, let us come to the ILO Convention No. 95, the date of which is 1949. We discover that its key article (Article 8) is partly reproduced as Article 4, Section 5, of the European Social Charter, about which we heard a good deal from the Minister. Both these remarkable documents that we are in danger of violating say nothing more than that deductions from wages shall be permitted only to the extent allowed by national laws, regulations, collective agreements or arbitration awards. If I may say so, it is difficult to see how such solemn trivia could be taken seriously by anyone who is not paid a fat fee to keep a straight face when they read it. In Britain, we already have written agreements of terms of employment, and we have put on employers the duty to itemise deductions from wages. We have appeals to industrial tribunals for unnotified deductions, and we have civil remedies before the county court. If more is necessary, it should not be difficult to graft it on to the Employment Protection (Consolidation) Act, so long as that inflated statute survives.

Bureaucratic bluff

Certainly a coherent solution to these problems cannot be cobbled together from the scraps of Truck Acts concerned with quite different, and now wholly extinct, practices. These Acts

---

[1] Lord Rochester as Liberal spokesman moved an amendment to delay the Second Reading until further consultations were completed.

will have to be abolished – there is no question of that. They will have to be repealed and obliterated before there can be new reconstruction. So why not call the bureaucratic bluff and repeal these old Acts? In the alarming jargon of international bureaucracy, I would urge the Government to 'denounce' the ILO Convention No. 95 and, for all I know, Conventions 1 to 94 at the same time in order to save postage. If we do inadvertently put the Government off-side in terms of international obligations, we should simply be generating more pressure to get on-side again, with up-to-date and relevant legislation.

Of course the Minister's advisers and the international bureaucrats have a great interest in mystifying us all and alarming us if we appear to be wanting to take what seem to be quite sensible steps. As Lord Orr-Ewing and Lord Selkirk said so forcefully, 20 years after the Karmel Committee urged repeal, the Liberal amendment seeks further to prolong delays. I have noticed before this tendency on the Liberal benches to shield behind caution and compromise as a pretext for indecision and inactivity. If we are serious in wanting progress, there are few better ways of encouraging the Government than by resisting this amendment and giving the Bill a Second Reading.

It is to the credit of a Conservative Government that on truck, as on other issues, it shows signs of awakening to the advantages of radical change. It is notable from the speeches we have had that the case for radical action came from the Conservative benches and the case for dragging our feet from Liberal and Labour speakers.

We are still paying a high price for our tardiness in adapting to new needs and new opportunities. I suggest that our attitude to this Bill and to this amendment should be taken as a measure of our readiness to turn our backs on nostalgia for the past and to rise to the challenge of still glittering prospects for economic and social progress. Unless Lord Rochester is so gracious and well-advised as to withdraw, I urge all those who do not owe him some loyalty to vote[1] against his equivocating amendment.

---

[1] On a Division, the amendment was lost and the Second Reading passed by 39 votes to 36. The Government subsequently agreed to denounce the ILO Convention in preparation for repealing the Truck Acts.

9. Closing Time

*Debate on a Question by the late Lord Spens asking whether
the Government will introduce flexible opening hours for
public houses in England and Wales on the Scottish model*

I CONGRATULATE Lord Spens in promoting a sober and interesting debate on the merits of more flexible opening hours. He has received support from the informal Repeal Group, which seeks to challenge outdated laws that restrict the freedom of adult citizens to live their own lives without hurting the like freedom of their neighbours. One test of whether legislation is outdated is to ask: If this law did not exist, would it be necessary to invent it? I believe the present licensing laws impose objectionable fetters on million of people that are not justified by any overriding imperatives of public policy.

Since some time ago the Tory Party appeared to cause confusion in the public mind between the peerage and what became known as the 'beerage', I think we should all declare an interest, or lack of interest, in this particular form of consumption. From the published figures I find I am well below the average annual consumption of 200 pints of beer per head of the population, although in wine I am safely between the annual average of 170 pints in France, and the 14 pints in the United Kingdom. Although I have never regularly taken advantage of the varied facilities of the 76,000 public houses and licensed hotels in the United Kingdom, I have to admit that on rare occasions I have been known to curse mildly because I could not find a single pub open at a time when it would have been convenient on a journey, on holiday or to celebrate a family or friendly reunion. I commend to your Lordships the thought of how much worse it must be for the millions of our fellow men who through work, or from choice, do not live their waking lives from approximately dawn until after dusk.

We have heard that the present licensing laws were introduced under emergency powers in the First World War, just as Tudor monarchs once clamped down on ale houses to encourage archery. I have no doubt that the stipulated 9 or 9½ hours of opening time between 11 a.m. and 10.30 p.m. or 11 p.m. generally suit the average convenience of the population. But the question I want to ask is why averages come into it? The average man does not play golf or visit Covent Garden or even indulge in hunting, shooting and fishing. It does not follow that strictly minority activities should be regulated by reference to average tastes or majority prejudices.

In one of the appendices to the excellent Erroll Report[1] there is a summary of an official survey into public attitudes towards licensing laws. It shows that about half of the random sample in 1970 favoured keeping opening hours as they were, and as they still are. But the other half was divided between a larger fraction favouring later closing and a smaller fraction preferring earlier closing. For a liberal democrat the only logical deduction from such a conflict of views is that the more flexible the hours of opening the larger the number of people who would get what they want.

Choice and variety for minorities

It is only in politics that we think it right for majorities constantly to impose their will on minorities. In the market-place, of which I am known to be an admirer, it is minorities that rule the roost all the time. Except for monopoly services such as the letter post, telephones, gas or electricity, almost everything we buy and where we choose to buy it reflects our individual preferences. In the cars we drive, in the clothes we wear, in the food we eat, we are all minorities. We would be voted down if we had to carry a democratic majority with us on every line of consumption.

I do not deny that all freedom is capable of abuse. We should, every one of us, be concerned that there are approaching 50,000 cases of drunken driving, but that remains a minute fraction of the 2½ million serious offences recorded by the police in a recent year. Although no more than 0·004 per cent of men are treated for alcoholism, we all know of others who are at risk. But the Erroll Report confirms our everyday observation that there is no simple correlation between excessive consumption and the number of hours that pubs are open, especially when drink can be so easily obtained for consumption at home. This lesson has not been disproved by experience in Scotland since the law was liberalised in 1976 and is upheld by evidence from places as far

[1] *Report of the Departmental Committee on Liquor Licensing*, Cmnd. 5154, HMSO, December 1972.

apart as Sweden and Australia, where severe restrictions on hours have not checked abuse. Nothing in the interesting sociological speculations of Lord Minto linked more flexible hours with proven excess. In the end he seemed to me to fall back into agnosticism.

I believe that we cannot make people better by legislation. That is the task for teaching, preaching, personal example and, in the last resort, enforceable laws against anti-social behaviour. It is clearly not a sin to drop in at the local. Indeed, no less an authority than the Director of the Christian Economic and Social Foundation, the Reverend George Brake, recently urged the need to preserve the place of the pub, which he thought 'the most favourable controlled environment for the consumption of alcohol'. He added:

'the well-managed public house provides a convenient controlled environment for drinking and is to be preferred to the uncontrolled situations in which drinking takes place at the present time'.

If the licensing laws were abolished, as I would wish, no pub would be required to open for more hours. Some pubs in some areas would no doubt preserve the present arrangements, while others elsewhere on some days or at some times of the year would open longer and later. The Erroll Report quotes the licensing authorities in London as granting 64,000 extensions in 1970, while a sample of 29 petty sessional divisions gave 28,000 exemption orders for an average of between an hour and an hour and a half of extra opening. No wonder the witnesses petitioning the Erroll Committee in favour of almost completely relaxing the law included the Metropolitan Commissioner of Police, as well as tourist boards and various catering and hotel organisations. There were of course then, as there will be again, familiar lobbies in favour of tighter controls. The question is: Who will speak for the millions of unorganised consumers?

I would argue that, whether any one of us would personally wish to take advantage of more flexible hours, we should not stand in the way of removing restrictions upon others with different preferences. Opening hours are no more a matter for majorities to override minorities than the times at which cinemas, restaurants or shops ply their trade between willing buyers and willing sellers. The contract that is implicit in a free society is that, even where our emotions are involved, we respect the choices, even the whims, of our fellow men as a condition for having our own differing tastes and values tolerated by others. If we admit that all freedoms are subject to abuse, we must acknowledge the need for penalties where excess may harm others. But such possibilities do not in my view justify the condescending paternalism, however well-intentioned, that tries to impose a selective morality by the crude, insensitive steam-roller of statutory prohibition.

10. RENT CONTROL

Debates on two motions by the late Lord Vaizey calling attention to the problems of housing, and moving the Second Reading of his Rent (Abolition of Control) Bill

I WOULD add my voice to that of Lord Robbins[1] and say I can think of no issue in political economy on which professional economists of widely differing tendencies are in more substantial agreement than on the unholy mess successive governments have made of the housing market. It is surely worth pondering that, despite the spending of mounting billions of pounds over half a century by governments of both Parties, housing has become a growing cause of human misery. I would go so far from the cross-benches as to argue that the so-called 'housing shortage' is largely the creation of politicians by their destruction and demolition of the market for rented accommodation.

It becomes a little easier almost week by week to assert the economist's basic proposition that prices do affect supply and demand. As we see with the EEC's Common Agricultural Policy, an artificially high price will increase supply and reduce demand, thereby creating an embarrassing surplus of farm products. In precisely the same way, rent control, by holding the price below the market level, will increase demand for accommodation, reduce the supply, and create the infamous housing shortage. I

[1] Until the illness leading to his death in 1984, Lord Robbins attended the House regularly as a cross-bencher and was a powerful voice in favour of economic liberalism.

am afraid the real handicap from which the occupants of the Labour benches suffer is that this kind of logic is simultaneously irresistible and unacceptable.

As others have said, rent control was introduced in 1915 as an emergency wartime measure. As a self-confessed market economist I have no difficulty in defending that kind of intervention. Indeed, as Lord Robbins has taught in his writings over many years, price control – and even rationing – are appropriate to a condition of siege, for one simple reason. Whereas a rise in price can generally be relied upon in an open market to call forth an increased supply that helps to redress the shortage, no such corrective is possible in the abnormal circumstances of war.

The trouble is that, instead of ending rent control with the end of the emergency that was its justification, successive governments have found it electorally profitable in the short run – which is the only run they know – to extend control and even to grant life tenancy into the second generation. As Lord Robbins has said, the ill-effects of drying up the supply were not immediately visible, simply because houses last a long time before they need replacing. But under rent control they just do not get replaced.

It is no wonder that politicians really thought that at last they had stumbled on a free lunch. They could indulge their favourite passion for doing good, or at least for feeling good, and at the same time serve their own electoral interest by collecting millions of grateful votes for keeping rents down. The cost was obligingly paid for by the landlords, who had conveniently little political weight.

We have heard about the injustices between prosperous tenants and often poorer landlords, and also between favoured tenants in controlled property and their unlucky neighbours forced into lengthening queues for council houses or into uncontrolled houses at inflated rents. The lesson of every country that has resorted to rent control has been that market forces are not so easily cheated. As the Francis Report[1] conceded back in 1971, the combination of low rents and security of tenure ensured that no new family houses were built for letting. Even worse, by holding rents below the rising cost of maintenance and

[1] *Rent Acts: Report of the Committee*, Cmnd. 4609, HMSO, 1971.

[43]

repair, especially in an age of inflation, political expediency has caused the decay and rapid decline in the number of houses under control. The statistics are remarkable. From a peak of 8½ million after the Second World War, the number of private tenancies fell to 4½ million in 1960 and to 2¾ million today.

The Bishop of Southwark spoke about the sorry sight of decay in New York. But New York is a classic case of the devastation created by rent control. It was indeed the universal phenomenon of devastation by rent control that produced a verdict from a Swedish professor, Assar Lindbeck, of sufficiently good Social Democratic credentials to appeal to Lord Roberthall. In his book, *The Political Economy of the New Left*, he wrote as follows:

'In many cases rent control appears to be the most efficient technique presently known to destroy a city – except for bombing'.

It is a by-product of this destructive policy that has caused governments to mount the treadmill of building houses to let at subsidised rents, in a vain effort to make good the shortage contrived by their own past follies. Others have spoken of the ill-effects on the mobility of labour, and I would underline an observation by Lord Vaizey[1] that rent control has forced many people into the market for buying a home when they would much prefer the convenience and flexibility of renting in a free market.

Direct help for the poor

The pretext for all of this costly and damaging policy has always been that poor families cannot afford market rents. But this is no new discovery. Poor families cannot afford sufficient food or sufficient clothing. It has been increasingly accepted, over a very long period, that the appropriate solution to this social problem of poverty is to top up their incomes in some way, not to fake the price system with all the consequent distortions of supply, demand, and consumer choice.

There is not time to go into alternative policies. My preference would be that of Lord Vaizey along the lines of straightforward repeal. We should sweep away the damaging rent controls as

---

[1] The untimely death of Lord Vaizey in 1984 at the age of 54 removed an outstanding liberal economist from the Conservative benches.

well as the wasteful, indiscriminate subsidies. We should address ourselves to people in need by introducing some coherent system of personal and portable housing allowances that would not be tied to staying-put in the same home. In my view, we should also phase out mortgage tax relief in return for progressive cuts in the rates of income tax.

In the past the partial and piecemeal efforts of Conservative governments to tackle these problems have been frustrated by what Lady Birk acknowledged was the 'threat' that the next Labour government would repeal any sensible measure in this field. I hope the remaining occupants on the dwindling Labour benches will forgive me for speaking frankly, but the emotional muddle of the last Labour Cabinet was revealed by a chastened Joel Barnett[1] in his remarkable recent memoir, *Inside the Treasury*,[2] which I commend to them. He wrote as follows:

'Talk of increasing council house rents and it was as if you were planning to snatch children from their mothers or put them to work down a mine'.

I sympathise with Mr Barnett because I know what it is like to be made to feel that kind of guilt. But to conclude on a more positive note, we should not allow that kind of mentality to obscure the merits of radical reform to remedy a housing problem that has been caused by an unholy mixture of misplaced benevolence, intellectual confusion and electoral opportunism.

10A. RENT CONTROL, AGAIN

I CONGRATULATE Lord Vaizey on bringing forward this Private Member's Bill to repeal the Rent Acts. His initiative has been encouraged by the non-party Repeal Group, following the debate which he opened in June last year. In that debate, all 11 speakers were in perfect agreement about the widespread human misery inflicted, especially on young people, by the difficulty or impossibility of finding a place to rent. Even more remarkable, four of the half-dozen professional economists in this House, speaking variously from the Conservative, Social Democrat and

[1] Since 1983 Lord Barnett.   [2] Andre Deutsch, London, 1982.

cross-benches, were found in rare unison emphasising that the major cause of the housing tragedy was rent control.

In the earlier debate, a notable contribution was made by my friend Lord Robbins from these cross-benches. Since he is tragically laid low by a most grievous stroke, I should like to quote three sentences from his speech.

> 'Rent control is essentially the fixing of maximum rents below the level which would prevail in a free market. Thus it affords an incentive to an excess of demand and a disincentive to spontaneous response of supply. This has occurred whenever and wherever it has been introduced'.

In a single sentence, it is a self-evident truism from elementary economic analysis that, in peace or war, in North or South, in houses or in ham sandwiches, if the price is held below the market-clearing level, the resulting excess of demand over supply will create a shortage. This prediction from basic theory is amply borne out by all the evidence.

More than 10 years ago the Institute of Economic Affairs, with which I must declare some connection, published a study entitled *Verdict on Rent Control*.[1] It assembled researches by leading international economists, including three Nobel Laureates, on countries as varied as Austria, France, Sweden, the United States and Britain. The introduction was written by a foremost British authority, the late Professor Fred Pennance, who entitled his essay 'Fifty Years, Five Countries, One Lesson'. The lesson was that rent control had done more harm than good by

> 'perpetuating shortages, encouraging immobility, swamping consumer preferences, fostering dilapidation of the housing stocks and eroding production incentives, distorting land-use patterns and the allocation of scarce resources'.

In every case studied, rent control was introduced as an emergency response to the disruption caused by war – after 1914 in Britain, Austria and France, and after 1940 in Sweden and the United States. Where control had been abolished, as in Sweden and most of the United States outside New York, the housing shortage had miraculously vanished. But wherever control has

---

[1] IEA Readings in Political Economy No. 7, 1972.

been perpetuated it has intensified the plight of people seeking even a temporary roof over their heads. For example, writing of rent control in Paris after 1945, the formidable, internationally famous philosopher Bertrand de Jouvenel concluded:

'It is self-perpetuating and culminates in both the physical ruin of housing and the legal dispossession of the owners. The havoc wrought here is not the work of the enemy but of our own measures'.

Evidence of dilapidation

In the debate last year, the Bishop of Southwark gave a rather depressing glimpse of what might politely be called the ineffable innocence of Church thinking on these wordly matters. He reported his shock at seeing the urban devastation in New York, which he implied was due to inadequate public spending. In truth, that devastation is directly due to the usual ravages of rent control. My authority is a Professor Peter Salins of the New York University Department of Urban Affairs. In 1980 he published a book called *The Ecology of Housing Destruction*, with a more revealing sub-title, 'The Economic Effects of Public Intervention in the Housing Market'. He showed that public spending of more than $10,000 million has not prevented the appalling deterioration and continuing destruction of the New York housing stock at the rate of 200,000 apartments every decade. In addition to reducing maintenance and construction, he showed that artificially depressed rents have increased demand and encouraged small families to occupy large premises. Professor Salins calls for the abolition of rent control and all its associated complexity of regulations. His conclusion on New York is, I believe, equally applicable to London and is as follows:

'There have been so many unsuccessful twists and turns along the path of well-intentioned tinkering that perhaps it is time to test the possibility that the generally reasonable incentives and disincentives of an unconstrained market might do a better job of allocating and conserving the housing stock'.

I draw precisely the same moral from the First Report of the House of Commons Environment Committee, which was published last year. Paragraphs 100 and 101 confirm that a major cause of the decline of the rented sector, from 7 million in 1945 to below 2 million today, was rent control and lifetime security of tenure. The impossibility of gaining repossession appears even more oppressive for small landlords than the derisory gross return of 2 or 3 per cent on their capital. Evidence was given that, in the decade since 1970, what are fraudulently called 'fair rents' doubled, while prices trebled and earnings quadrupled.

Baroness Birk: *I think Lord Harris must agree that the whole situation in New York is entirely different from that in London. In New York you have apartments with very high rents. Has he seen some of the properties that people are renting at the lower end of the scale? I imagine that he is talking about property around Manhattan and that sort of area. Certainly nowhere in his quotations from the report of the Environment Committee does it state that a repeal of the rent control Acts would improve or increase the quantity of rented housing. In fact, when the Committee discuss it they point out what has happened and also what would happen if this was reversed – that it would not make the situation better, but in fact would make it worse.*

Lord Harris: The whole of Professor Salins's report on New York concentrates on places like the Bronx. He is concerned with the poor end of the market in New York and not with Manhattan.

In the House of Commons Committee report, to which I have referred, paragraph 101 says that

'Most witnesses argued that a revival of supply in the [rented] sector would require the removal or reduction of rent and security controls, together with a growth of confidence that future changes in legislation and government policy would not reimpose tighter controls'.

Baroness Birk: *Would he mind reading the following sentence?*

Lord Harris: Not at all. It reads:

'However, many felt that even this could not succeed and removal of controls would simply exacerbate housing stress without achieving acceptable housing conditions for those in the sector'.

Baroness Birk: *Thank you.*

Lord Harris: But they say that the *majority* of witnesses gave the earlier view, and the witnesses included Shelter, the Small Landlords Association, Professor Donnison, Brighton Borough

Council, the City of Manchester Council, Chestertons, and the Paddington Federation of Tenants and Residents Associations. I am establishing that no clear-cut view is handed down from the House of Commons report. It is all open for argument, and we propose to continue that argument.

From the evidence in that report I was surprised to discover that those who derive much satisfaction from baiting the landlords and working up prejudice in this matter, argue that rents may be held low but the owners would gain from increased property values over a period of years. Yet in practice it is elsewhere acknowledged that a house with a sitting tenant might be lucky to fetch 20 per cent of its market value with vacant possession. The whole point is that it is just such grotesquely falsified values which provide less scrupulous owners with a strong temptation to neglect repairs and get sitting tenants out.

Leaving aside the immorality of rent control, which I think should trouble its defenders rather more, the down-to-earth economic question is whether repeal would bring more lettings onto the market at rents people can afford. I believe that clear evidence is provided by the orchestrated complaints about 'loopholes', which take the form of holiday homes, company lettings, licences and shared occupancy in place of full tenancies. The success of these escape clauses in my view provides proof beyond any doubt whatever that, where the legalised theft of the Rent Acts can be avoided, new accommodation is forthcoming to relieve the distress of homelessness.

The best way to end the 'loopholes' is simply to repeal these obstructive statutes by supporting Lord Vaizey's Bill in the Lobby.[1] The way to help the poor is not to control rents any more than it is to control the price of food or clothing. To distort the price system obstructs supply and demand, as we see to our cost in a quite different connection with the Common Agricultural Policy.

Social versus economic policy

In conclusion, I would emphasise that poverty is the proper province of social policy and is best tackled by topping-up low

---

[1] The debate on the Second Reading was adjourned and no vote was taken.

incomes in some form. It should not be confused with general economic policy nor with policy on particular prices. Alas! It has to be said that for decades the Labour Party has won votes by confounding these wholly distinct issues to the detriment of both economic and social progress. It has further obstructed reform by reckless threats to restore or even to extend rent control, as we have been reminded that Mr Crosland did – to his eternal shame – in 1974 by destroying the market for rented furnished premises. I take some encouragement that, now the Labour Party looks like being reduced to talking to itself, a special responsibility shifts to the Social Democrats as the alternative government of the future. It only needs David Owen and the eagerly awaited Lord Grimond to teach the Liberals some economic sense for the repeal of rent control to open up the way for long-term reconstruction of the much-needed market in rented accommodation.

11. THE COAL MONOPOLY

*Debate on a motion by Lord Ezra calling for
a long-term energy strategy*

WE MUST all have been impressed by the wide-ranging opening speech by Lord Ezra. As with other orations from the Liberal benches, I found myself wondering what link it had with the fundamental principles of liberal philosophy. I shall try to remedy this deficiency by warning against pinning too-high hopes on a long-term energy strategy. He displayed a wide knowledge gained from a lifetime of some 35 years in the coal industry. I hope, however, he will bear in mind that a lot of knowledge can be a dangerous thing, unless informed by constant humility about the changing variables which can never be known in advance.

The complaint might be made that we have suffered by not having a long-term energy strategy over recent decades. Yet the question I want to pose is: Who could have foreseen the dramatic transformation of supply and demand in the United Kingdom and indeed in the world energy market? In 1960 coal represented almost 100 per cent of British fuel production and we relied for some 30 per cent of our consumption on imported oil. By 1973, despite the eruption of natural gas, we relied on imports for one-half of our then substantially increased consumption. When we come to 1982 we find that, with North Sea oil in full spate, we produced a surplus of fuel to export while coal accounted for no more than one-third of our total production. Could any long-term fuel strategy have predicted such far-reaching changes?

If we have survived without too much difficulty, it is thanks chiefly to the adaptation of production and consumption to price adjustments in the market – a market, I may say, made more imperfect by government obstructions and intervention. Allowing for the long time-lags for producers and consumers to adjust their supply and demand from one fuel to another, is it not astonishing that we have avoided disaster without Lord Ezra's strategy? Indeed, at intervals since 1973, the only disruption has been caused or threatened by the coal industry which, as I shall try to argue, has suffered from the handicap of a long-term plan.

The folly of the *Plan for Coal,* as with all similar political aspirations, is that it was an example of physical planning without too much regard for changing prices. I recall a speaker in our recent debate on unemployment urging government planning on the analogy of private enterprise companies which, as we all know, may plan for five or 10 years ahead. But competitive planning by separate companies is quite a different matter from centralised government planning. No company pretends to plan for the whole industry, and it certainly does not inscribe its targets on tablets of stone.

All business planning is tentative and conditional upon changes in the market-place. Each firm estimates the future market and its likely share, but then stands ready to adapt to unexpected changes. Competition provides a perpetual feedback of movements in relative prices reflecting substitution of new sources of supply. If things turn out worse than expected, enterprising businessmen are ready to lower their prices to sell their current production, and to cut back their plans for the future.

National or corporatist planning stands in the sharpest contrast. For a start, it will always include a large dash of political expediency. Its targets will often smack more of hopes than of practical realities. Secondly, government plans are cast in terms of physical quantities that extrapolate forward from past

[51]

experience in a way which has been compared with trying to steer a boat by looking backwards at the wake. Thirdly, once government has set its seal on a plan, it takes on a life of its own and becomes highly rigid. It is then likely to be persisted in long after the assumptions on which it was based have been falsified by changing circumstances. Above all, official plans or strategies give hostages to fortune. They raise expectations among favoured interests and so provide a breeding ground for bitterness when the expectations are not fulfilled.

The need for competition

So we come to the *Plan for Coal*. By far the best obituary was written by Professor Colin Robinson and his colleague, Eileen Marshall, in their evidence to the recent Select Committee on European Coal Policy. They pointed out that the past decade 'should have provided a favourable environment for the British coal industry'. In 1973 the Arab oil cartel handed coal a massive competitive advantage. So the plan in 1974 projected an optimistic target, centred on production of 135 million tonnes for 1985 and based on a government commitment to a large-scale investment programme. Success of this plan depended upon a 4 per cent annual increase in average output per man to be achieved in part by closing down high-cost pits and opening up new, lower-cost capacity.

Despite Mr Scargill's Marxist-Leninist mathematics, the investment of £7,000 million is the only part of the plan to have been fulfilled. Output per man, assisted by the bonus scheme and the 1979 tax cuts, has increased by an annual average of nearer 1 per cent than the promised 4 per cent, largely because the closure of high-cost pits lagged behind the programme until Sir Norman Siddall's surgery last year.

Behind Mr Scargill's inflammatory and ideological rhetoric lies the damning truth that British deep-mined coal, at a cost averaging £46 a tonne after subsidies, costs twice or three times as much as the best achieved in the United States or Australia. But the paradox is that, by protecting British coal against imports and by raising subsidies, governments have weakened the very competitive pressures that would have made for more efficiency. They have thereby enabled the National Union of Mineworkers

[52]

to keep pushing average costs up much faster than the cost-of-living index. In short, the *Plan for Coal* inflated the monopoly power of Mr Scargill and of his predecessor to obstruct adaptation to market changes, to milk the taxpayer, and to impose higher prices on consumers – including housewives, industry and the captive Central Electricity Generating Board.

I believe that our best strategy is to get markets to operate more freely and more flexibly. As the National Coal Board's outstanding marketing director, Malcolm Edwards, never tires of repeating, the best way to check imports, to stop more nuclear power stations and to speed conversion from oil in industry and electricity generating, is to produce a dependable supply of British coal at £30 to £35 a tonne. That simply means a lot less coal produced at £50 to £80 a tonne, which now requires the public to pour in capital and current subsidies which are equivalent to approaching £150 a week for every miner in the industry.

I share the view expressed by other speakers that there is great hope for the future of British coal. But it is a hope that can be fulfilled only if the price of coal is made competitive and customers can rely on an uninterrupted supply, without the costly insurance policy of massive stocks or keeping alternative generating capacity in reserve. There is no future for British coal under Mr Scargill's political programme of high costs and unreliable delivery.

For the good of coal miners and their customers, our strategy should be to break up the present politicised monopoly, phase out the subsidies, and find ways of giving workers a personal equity in the success of their own efforts. As a first step towards such a competitive strategy, I want to offer the Minister a simple proposal. It is that the Government should repeal Section 1(1)(a) of the 1946 Nationalisation Act which gave the National Coal Board the exclusive power to work all new discoveries of coal found in Great Britain. I believe we would soon find that there is nothing like competition, even the threat of competition, to galvanise a monopoly into greater efficiency.

PART III:
Markets, Taxation and Equality

12. UP WITH THE MARKET

*Debate on a motion by Lord Beswick calling attention to
the effects of over-reliance on market forces*

I SHOULD like to try to explain in very general terms why I
consider that Her Majesty's Government are so far from
deserving the well-worn strictures as a band of extremists hell-
bent on turning the clock back to the heyday of 19th-century
liberalism. I believe that these charges show the danger of
politicians being misled by their own rhetoric, and sometimes
by the rather robust rhetoric we have from some members of the
Government.

Over many years we have heard a popular fiction, especially
dear to Liberals and Social Democrats, that since the war public
policy has oscillated between the opposing poles of two dis-
tinctive ideologies. From where I sit on the cross-benches, it
seems nearer the truth that, in the balance between market and
government, the pendulum that we used to hear about has
increasingly been replaced by the ratchet.

Since 1945 – I would argue in many respects since 1906 –
party politics has seen a cumulative, if you will, a progressive,
shift away from the dispersed initiative of ordinary people in the
competitive market and towards increasingly centralised direc-
tion, bureaucratic control and pervasive state power. To my
imagination politicians often seem like mediaeval knights, with
multiplying bands of retainers, all clad in such a weight of
armour as to be deprived of the flexibility necessary for effective
action. Thus in office they appear to wield great power, and yet
so often in practice have proved impotent to achieve their most
basic aims.

I think it right that this House should pay attention to the wisdom of the past. I therefore bring you some words written more than 200 years ago by Adam Smith, when he warned politicans against excessive intervention, in attempting which he said:

'they must always be exposed to innumerable delusions, and for the proper performance of which no human wisdom or knowledge could ever be sufficient . . .'.

On this issue of the general superiority of the market it is not sufficiently understood that Keynes was more frequently in some agreement with his classical forbears. Significantly for this debate, in 1926 he wrote an essay, entitled 'The End of Laissez-faire', in which he stated:

'Capitalism, wisely managed, can probably be made more efficient for attaining economic ends than any alternative yet in sight'.

That was in 1926. Lest it be thought that his *General Theory* changed all that, I should like to quote from his best-known work in 1936, when he wrote:

'The advantage to efficiency of the decentralisation of decisions and of individual responsibility is even greater perhaps than the 19th century supposed; and the reaction against the appeal to self-interest may have gone too far'.

If that were true almost 50 years ago, how much further have we now strayed down the wrong road? So I would ask: Where is the excessive reliance on market forces that haunts the Labour benches? Take the labour market. It is perfectly true that the ending of prices and incomes policy has permitted much more flexibility for managements and men to adapt to changing economic realities. But there remains a fearful incubus of trade union monopoly power and legal privileges, added to what now appears the hollow mockery of 'employment protection' laws, wages councils, rent controls, and, above all, the confused and conflicting operation of high taxes, social benefits and all kinds of subsidies that make it profitable for thousands of people to choose unemployment rather than work.

Public versus private sector

On top of all that, approaching a third of the entire labour force is locked up in the public sector, mostly cushioned from the invigoration of market forces, and the results for over-manning and inefficiency are increasingly visible and indeed widely acknowledged. Before the eruption of Mr Wedgwood Benn, the Labour Party saw itself essentially as a moderate movement. Yet by 1979 it had brought about far more extensive nationalisation in Britain than in such model social democracies as Sweden or West Germany.

The essence of a market economy is not simply the private ownership of industry, as some of its defenders imagine. The essence of a market economy is that production is guided by competition between alternative suppliers to serve the changing demands of consumers at home or abroad. The really fatal flaw of nationalised industry is that governments, for political expediency, seek to shield it from competition, knowing that the domestic consumers or taxpayers can always be made to pay, no matter how high costs may rise.

The contrast between public and private industry stands out more starkly today than ever before. At a time when private industry has been compelled by hated market forces to transform productivity, we see a lagging performance in many of the nationalised monopolies: I would say in railways, coal, and postal services – and I am not enamoured of gas and electricity. An instructive contrast is that where even a nationalised industry is faced by market forces in the form of foreign competition – as in steel, motor cars, or shipbuilding – determined management has been able to achieve some of the glittering prizes being won by private industry.

I readily agree with the critics here and elsewhere who say that market forces do not operate with anything approaching perfection. But I would strongly argue that the well-intended effort to remove every blemish has invariably led to a far worse situation. In a fastidious endeavour to cure a skin rash we have spread a bubonic plague of bureaucratic regulation into every crevice of the economy. One result is a standard tax rate, including national insurance, of 40 to 50 per cent on wages as low as one-third of average earnings. A quite different kind of outcome, which we shall witness in this debate, is the politicisation of every aspect of economic affairs, with increasing contention and bitterness which in the world outside has led to a declining respect for politicians and indeed for the law. It is true

[56]

that the market economy requires a framework of law for its operation, but that is a far cry from the present legal straitjacket into which it is clamped in so many respects.

I therefore conclude by saying that if the Social Democrats really want to break the mould they might start ostentatiously by burying the old consensus that has got us into so much difficulty. They might then join the intellectual vanguard of economists and others, including many disillusioned socialists, who are endeavouring to redefine a new public philosophy of limited but effective government that works with the grain of market forces. 'Market forces' are the only way of describing ordinary men and women as consumers and producers, co-operating in competition to their mutual benefit. When members are not in this House to tell us about the cold and crude concept of the market, they go about their business as part of these market forces outside.

I conclude by urging the Government to continue moving more decisively towards the market, which is not only most fully consistent with individual freedom and responsibility but, as a direct consequence, offers the best springboard to lasting economic recovery.

13. Down With Taxes

Debate on a motion by Lord Boyd-Carpenter calling for urgent liberation of resources for the creation of wealth and the reduction of high taxation

THE MOTION in the name of Lord Boyd-Carpenter exactly reflects my own impatience with the failure of the Government to push on more rapidly in reducing the burden of taxation which has grown remorselessly throughout the whole of this century. If we look back to 1900 we find that government took 15 per cent of the national income. By 1938 it took 30 per cent of the national income, by 1960 40 per cent and, through the 1970s, around 50 per cent. I checked back with the Blue Book for 1982 which showed that total state spending was then £128,000 million out of a net national income of £240,000 million. Those two figures tell us that central and local government and their various offshoots laid claim to 53 per cent of all the income earned by the exertions and enterprise of this nation.

In a prudent world this mounting public spending has to be financed from rates and a whole variety of taxes, or it has to be borrowed from current savers and eventually repaid by future taxpayers. It must be obvious, even to such overflowingly generous and well-intentioned people as Lord Beswick, that there is some limit to the amount of tax that governments can take without doing more harm than good. This is a matter of judgement. Unlike Lord Barnett, I judge that we have already gone beyond the bounds of prudence.

I would assert that, above a modest level, all taxes damage our economic performance in a variety of ways. Most people, despite what Lord Beswick has said, do not positively rejoice in paying higher taxes. There is no such thing as a free tax. We all know that, as local authority rates have rocketed, firms have been forced out of socialist city centres and sometimes, too often, have been forced out of business.

Lord Beswick: *I did not talk about rejoicing in paying higher taxes. I rejoiced that we had a system which could give the surgical treatment which a poor man needed. Does not the speaker also rejoice in that; and, if he does rejoice, does he not accept that it follows that we must pay taxes?*

Lord Harris: Lord Beswick implied that people should take pleasure in paying taxes because it led to some good things of which they approved. I approve of some things the Government does, but I thoroughly disapprove of many other things where I can see that my money is wasted. So I cannot take pleasure in the total burden of tax that falls upon me. My argument is that income tax and national insurance contributions raise costs, depress efficiency, distort effort, make British products less competitive than foreign competition and so destroy jobs.

I was not impressed by the complacent comparison of Lord Barnett with European tax levels – and for a number of reasons. In the first place, the structure of our own income tax is more onerous, especially on lower and higher incomes. Secondly, European earnings over the post-war years have risen a good deal faster than those in Britain; so that, despite rising taxes, take-home pay has also risen faster. Furthermore, Britain suffers from larger handicaps than France, Germany or even Sweden, especially in our troublesome trade unions and in the more extensive nationalisation. Therefore, we need all the additional help that we can get from lower taxes.

It is a fallacy to suppose that taxes do not matter because only some people are affected by their disincentive impact. Lord Barnett conceded that some people are so discouraged; the only dispute is how widely that particularly damaging effect runs. I wholly agree with Lord Barnett in his attack on taxes on lower income. Before the war working-class families like my own parents never paid taxes unless incomes rose to something like two or three times average earnings. Today income tax starts for many at levels nearer one-third of average earnings, and even below the entitlement to supplementary benefit. It is no wonder that we hear of the unemployment trap and the poverty trap where people are discouraged from taking a job which would leave them worse off, after loss of tax and benefits, than if they stayed on social security. As Lord Barnett acknowledged quite explicitly, we are literally taxing people into poverty and unemployment as well as taxing other people into the black market or the underground economy.

Spending other people's money

Another count against this great tax snatch is that, by knocking-off almost 40 per cent from take-home pay, workers are encouraged to try to pass the buck to their employers by demanding wage and salary increases which firms cannot afford. The buck eventually has to stop somewhere, and it tends to stop on the backs of the creators of wealth. It is indisputable that all taxes are a negative transfer of goods and services away from individuals and towards government. The trouble is that higher taxes must, however, marginally, reduce the flow of wealth which alone enables us to pay increasing taxes in the future.

A further disadvantage of high public spending which has not been touched upon is that no government can give as good value for our money as we get when we spend it for ourselves and our families. The men in Whitehall cannot know and cannot really even care about individual preferences which differ very widely. They are inevitably inclined to spend other people's money just as though it was other people's money. A Minister in this House for whom I have a great deal of admiration was nevertheless reported in *Hansard* as saying:

'I rather like spending other people's money; it is one of the most enjoyable functions of a Minister's life'.

At that time I was deeply shocked. That was four years ago. Now I am a hundred years older and wiser and sadder; and I have come to accept that there is not much prospect of getting politicians to treat the taxpayer's money with the most especial respect it should deserve.

Even if Ministers were recruited exclusively from the legendary one-armed Aberdonians with sewn-up pockets, I would argue that it is impossible for public services to be as cost-conscious as private suppliers who have to compete to win customers. Even in this recession, we have seen that managements in local government, in education, and in health services have faced none of the market disciplines which have compelled private enterprise to improve efficiency by cutting out waste, ending slack working habits, and reducing manpower often by 10, 20 or 30 per cent, without in many cases reducing output or capacity. The additional difficulty which has been touched upon is that state services and nationalised industries breed overpowerful trade unions that have fought, often without scruple, to retain every over-manned post and preserve every demarcation and restrictive practice. I heard Lord Ezra say that the National Coal Board has won Queen's Awards for some of its technical triumphs; but it would win no taxpayers' or customers' awards for its efficiency or its return on capital over a period of years.

The trouble fundamentally is that, wherever any activity is plugged into government, all the pressures are for more spending. Lord Barnett would agree, I know, with this proposition in the light of his own excellent post-mortem on the years 1974 to 1979 when he was Labour's Chief Secretary of the Treasury. His remarkably readable requiem, entitled *Inside the Treasury*, is full of instructive revelations which I never cease to advertise. If his sales are doing well it is partly due to my advocacy. Early in his book he lamented:

'The days had long since passed when I naively thought it

would be easy to persuade my colleagues that two plus two really did make four'.

A little later he said:

> 'So many of my colleagues wanted to have their cake and eat it; even the most intelligent of them wanted both tax cuts and public expenditure increases'.

I think his Labour colleagues are not so different from many Ministers on the other side of the House. But I think I can say with some confidence that at least the present Government has not been guilty of that degree of folly. I have no doubt that the Chancellor would like to get spending and taxes down, even if Mr Peter Walker and other Tory rustics and romantics are not entirely in agreement. I would therefore urge Mr Nigel Lawson to persevere, and I offer this concluding thought: no single boon would do more for growth and employment prospects than a large and continuing reduction in the burden of taxation on workers, savers and investors. It is they – millions of ordinary and extraordinary people, not governments of any party – who are the true source of Britain's wealth and future prosperity.

14. GOODBYE TO EQUALITY

Debate on a motion by Lord Longford calling for greater equality

I DO not know Lord Longford enough to judge whether his amiable qualities include absent-mindedness. But I have a special reason for hoping that he forgets to withdraw his 'motion for papers' at the end of this debate.[1] I have been wondering what papers we could recommend to advance his education – not more Blue Books, not more Fabian tracts or official reports, of which he may have swallowed too many. What other papers would cheer him and help persuade him that his plea for 'greater equality' has already gone a long way towards being fulfilled in our lifetime by the remarkable operations of private enterprise in

---

[1] Debates are staged in the House of Lords in the form of a motion 'calling for Papers' on the chosen topic. The mover concludes the debate by withdrawing his request for papers.

competitive markets? My choice of papers to put this debate into perspective would be the social commentaries embodied in bound volumes, not of *Hansard*, but of such journals as *Homes and Gardens, Good Housekeeping, Woman's Weekly*, and all those contemporary magazines on holidays, motoring, eating out, foreign travel and other growing national pastimes.

Who now remembers the working-class world in which at least some of us were brought up? Who remembers the world of fly-papers, of gas coppers and black-leaded grates, of mangles and meat safes, of boiled milk in the summer and acres of lino – or should I say linoleum? Such domestic horrors have now been banished by aerosols, detergents, washing-machines, heaters of all kinds, fitted kitchens, refrigerators, deep freezes and wall-to-wall carpeting. Critics can dwell on sad exceptions, but the lives of most ordinary people have been transformed in two generations. I am arguing – and I think it a fair point from the cross-benches – that none of this practical progress owes very much at all to politicians and governments.

The larger part of government social spending consists in taking money from the majority of people and returning it to much the same people in cash and kind – minus heavy freight charges in both directions. While the forbears of many members here were calling for the 'elevation of the masses', the practical process of improvement was being advanced by businessmen, galvanised by unequal incentives in the market, to find better ways of serving their consumers and, at the same time, offering more rewarding employment. The whole history of liberal capitalism is one of extending the luxuries of a privileged minority ever wider to become the everyday conveniences, even necessities, of growing majorities. The tragedy of the last 100 years is that the market worked so well that we took it for granted and began to make its operations more difficult.

It has been said that in confronting social policy we should be 'inspired by love but guided by reason'. My reasoning tells me that many noble intentions aired in debates such as this are likely to finish up doing more harm than good. Our concern should not be with the distracting and destructive phantom of equality. It should be with a realistic discussion of how we can revive our economy so as to afford a more humane minimum standard for those who cannot maintain themselves in the market. We would all agree that no-one should be allowed to fall below what we judge an acceptable poverty level. But I want to ask why today's conception of a minimum standard is so much above what I will call the 'skimmed-milk standard' that was applied by Booth and Rowntree in their poverty surveys 100 years ago? The improvement owes far less to the second-hand generosity of politicians, doling out other people's money, than to the application of capital and labour in multiplying marketable output.

More discriminating welfare benefits

It is clear that 'greater equality' has a powerful emotional and even aesthetic appeal for its advocates. But its danger lies in the conflict with the indispensable requirement of incentives for a free and efficient society. My argument in a nutshell is that the disincentive cost of the British welfare state has now become the major obstacle to spreading prosperity through the more effective operation of vigorous competitive enterprise. I agree with the tendency of much of the remarks of Lord Young of Dartington. I express them in this way: our mistake in social policy has been that instead of concentrating help selectively on those in need – for example, as he said, by a reverse income tax – British policy has indulged the essentially collectivist folly of universal free services and benefits which are both inefficient to the recipient and inordinately expensive to the taxpayer as provider. That is why we now have at the same time excessive taxation going hand in hand with inadequate help for some categories of special need.

The burden of indiscriminate benefits is damaging in a host of ways. I shall mention briefly four. First, high taxes necessarily inflate labour costs, at the same time as they deflate the incentives to effort and enterprise. Secondly, the availability of universal services puts a premium on sloth and safety-first. Thirdly, the spreading burden of taxes down the income scale impoverishes millions of families who thereby become dependent upon multiplying state subsidies. And finally – for the moment – the narrowing or non-existent gap between taxed income from work and untaxed social benefits must increase voluntary unemployment and so reduce real output.

[63]

Sceptics will find much more interesting evidence than provided in the Diamond Reports[1] in a recent compilation by Ralph Howell, MP, entitled *Why Work?*. Why indeed, when taxation on a family of a man, wife and two children starts at a wage of £41 a week, compared with tax-free supplementary benefits on offer at £66 a week? Why work indeed, when the head of that family would need to earn £115 a week to be better of than collecting unemployment benefit plus tax refunds? Why work indeed, when the same breadwinner in a family of four earning £105 a week comes out of the tax-benefit mangle only £11 better off than if he earned £35 a week? Greater equality? No – not unless we want, in Churchill's phrase, 'equal sharing of miseries' rather than 'unequal sharing of blessings'.

I conclude that, instead of sliding with Lord Longford down the slippery slope of equality, we should urgently seek to reduce the half of national income now spent by government, to cut taxes and to widen differences of income from both work and investment. We should in my view pursue a deliberate policy of differential incentives in the long-run interests not least of the poor and the handicapped. If we really want to encourage employment and enliven our economy, we need above all to free this economy from decades of self-inflicted political mutilation.

[1] *Royal Commission on the Distribution of Income and Wealth* (Chairman: Lord Diamond): Report No. 6: *Lower Incomes*, Cmnd. 7175, HMSO, May 1978, Ch. 4.